Faces, Places & Cases

Real NCIS History

by Tricia Mansell

Faces, Places & Cases

Real NCIS History

By Special Agent Tricia Mansell

*(Photo: NCIS Operation Red Blanket
Italy - 1982)*

Faces, Places & Cases (c) 2021 Real NCIS History **Mansell Publishing** all rights reserved. No part of this book may be used or reproduced in any manner without written permission from the author, except in the case of brief quotations embodied in critical articles or reviews. Also, except permission is not required for use (oral or written) by any person who is a present or former employee of NCIS. Address inquiries to **Mansell Publishing** at ndmansell@gmail.com

Printed in the United States of America.

First Edition

ISBN: 9798508915650

TABLE of CONTENTS

Introduction   page 1

Chapter 1: **Recognition of Leaders**   page 7

Chapter 2: **Early History & the Evolution of NCIS**   page 15

Chapter 3: **VIETNAM**   page 41

Chapter 4: **NCIS Expansions Employees / Methodology**   page 49

Chapter 5: **Criminal Cases**   page 77

Chapter 6: **Foreign Counterintelligence**   page 91

Chapter 7: **Places**   page 109

Chapter 8: **Special Agent Afloat (SAA)**   page 127

Chapter 9: **Terrorism & Protective Service**   page 137

"A Moment in Time"   page 151

Caricatures   page 173

In Appreciation

When trying to edit his / her own work, a writer often sees what is supposed to be there, and not actually what is there. For additional editing assistance I turned to my husband Ed and daughter Charlotte. I want to recognize their efforts and offer great appreciation to each of them.

Note: This is **NOT** an official publication of the Naval Criminal Investigative Service (NCIS).

Information herein comes from either researching years of historical documents saved by NCIS employees, or from open media sources.

Historical information was sent to author for purposes of research, writing or editing, and publication.

All information is unclassified. There is no current or sensitive information.

This book explores the foundation of NCIS, and provides personal accounts of cases and operations, including people involved and activity locations.

If any reader finds corrections that should be made, author will be happy to make same in future editions. Note that photographs were hard to come by, and in some cases age has degraded them.

The author's intent was to both provide an account for NCIS employees as a memoir, and to provide a readable story for anyone to enjoy. Therefore, language and abbreviations found in the NCIS workplace were adjusted accordingly.

INTRODUCTION

I was employed by the Naval Criminal Investigative Service (NCIS) for a dozen years in the latter 1970s and all of the 1980s. I was hired as a Special Agent, and after years of working in that regard, chose to become a Foreign Counterintelligence (FCI) Analyst. This civilian career followed my serving on active duty as a naval intelligence officer.

Years later I joined an association of former or retired NCIS employees, and for a few years edited an in-house magazine. I often contributed stories to this magazine. Years after that I was asked to write either a book or a commemorative magazine on the history of NCIS. I wrote a first draft, which was never published, but gave me the opportunity to do extensive research and fact-finding for such a project. Years later I decided to publish this history.

ORGANIZATION NAME

As the reader will note, the history of NCIS goes back well over 50 years, and actually stretches into one hundred years. These years have brought changes in the mission, organizational structure, and name, and so for clarity I will use NCIS within the book in every case unless otherwise inappropriate.

INFORMATION

This book is NOT an official publication. In order to preclude reference to any NCIS missions which may still be sensitive or classified, there is not a single reference in this book after the year 2016; most information within goes back decades. The active NCIS organization was not contacted, consulted or asked to supply any information for this book. That said, this is a *true* collection of history and memories.

I received information from members sent to me personally for publication, both when I edited the magazine, and when I did research for a book. Additionally I was furnished historical information in the form of numerous CDs from retired NCIS agents **Vic McPherson** and **Neill Roberts,** who advised they had collected this through the years. They also advised that retired agents **Troy Gillespie** and **Blair Gluba** were very instrumental in building this historical data base. Some information I received directly from retired agent **McPherson**, who spent hours combing through naval archives for declassified historical materials. I see no need for footnotes; all information can be found in above sources. All photographs used in this book have been previously published, within NCIS materials, with the permission of the subject.

Everything written in this book is unclassified. If it was ever classified it has been declassified and marked accordingly. I consider this as a book I have mostly *curated (not written)* based on my research and selection of materials others have documented through the years. I include very few of my own personal memories.

If the reader wants to learn more about NCIS history, one good place to start is an online web recently created for collection of such history. It is open to the public and can be found at **https://ncisahistory.org**

NCIS AGENTS

Of those mentioned in this book, some are now deceased, many are retired, and perhaps a few are still actively employed. During the period from writing - to printing - to purchasing this book, some will change categories. In consideration of these factors every special agent will be referred to as Special Agent or (SA.)

CASE AGENTS

Cases are usually controlled by one agent, but often worked with the assistance of many agents. Names of SAs involved at the local, regional, and/or NCIS Headquarters (HQ) level are listed if known, but in many cases that information is not readily available. No disrespect is intended.

CONTENT SELECTION

Articles were chosen which fall within the information parameters mentioned above. Additionally, choices were made to include examples of memories or missions of a specific era. Apologies to any and all whose stories are not included; perhaps you think they should have been, and you are probably right, but of the many thousands that exist, hopefully a "like" representation is in this book.

This book contains information collected and/or written by many with love, respect, and deep loyalty to NCIS. Each is desirous of keeping memories alive for the benefit of all. Thanks go out to specific SAs mentioned above, and each and to every contributor mentioned herein.

NCIS GROWTH

It would take many people many months to properly analyze the growth of NCIS, and no doubt such a process is well underway. That said, after reading thousands of documents it is possible for me to make some educated comments.

In terms of mission focus NCIS grew organically to satisfy the needs of the naval department. Anyone with a military background knows that military members are a microcosm of society; and crime seen within the military mirrors current society.

-The 1960s began with emphasis on background investigations, but ended with a growing need for criminal investigations, and involvement in the war zone of Vietnam.

-The 1970s closed out the Vietnam office, but elsewhere emphasis was growing in the criminal fields of large-scale thefts, narcotics use, and drug trafficking.

-The 1980s has been aptly named the *Decade of the Spy.* Before the winding down of the Soviet Union, the Soviets and their satellite countries were heavily targeting our naval forces, and for various reasons, all at once these spy activities came to light. By the end of the 1980s terrorism had some concern, and forensic science and jointly linked data bases significantly changed investigations.

-The 1990s began with war and continued with a focus on terrorists of Middle Eastern origin, and also included an active pursuit of *cold cases.*

-The 2000s until present have been in response to the massive terror attack of *9/11* (September 11, 2001) and in the war zones that followed. Also, there has been a growing unease in the world about who America's friends and enemies really are. For purposes of counter-intelligence those at play include Russia, some of the Middle East, North Korea, and China. With the expansion and dependence on technology, *cyber security* has become a top priority.

-The agency growth included increasing the numbers of NCIS agents on deployed warships, agent deployments in war zones, expansion of protective service (bodyguard) details, anti-piracy efforts at sea, and establishment of cold case units to capitalize on new vision and advances in science.

Structurally NCIS has grown from a department within the Office of Naval Intelligence to an organization directly under the Secretary of the Navy. NCIS expanded from an organization of only agents and secretaries, to now include hundreds of support personnel, due to the addition of analysts and various technicians.

Lastly, many in the agent corps of NCIS through the years came from active military service and/or law enforcement jobs. The remaining came from a wide assortment of backgrounds. All came from widely scattered geographic areas. The *language skills, cultural knowledge, goals, experiences, leadership, training and talents* each brought to NCIS, collectively served to enhance mission accomplishments.

Tricia Mansell

Chapter 1: **Recognition of Leaders**
Senior Military Leaders

CAPTAIN JACK O. JOHNSON, USNR
February 1966 - July 1966

CAPTAIN BARNEY MARTIN, USN
June 1973 - June 1976

CAPTAIN EDWARD G. RIFENBURGH, USN
July 1966 - July 1970

CAPTAIN LEWIS EDWARD CONNELL, USN
April 1976 – 1979

CAPTAIN JOHN Q. EDWARDS, USN
August 1970 - June 1973

CAPTAIN JOSEPH "JERRY" SORIANO, USN 1979 – 1982

CAPTAIN PERRY D. HOSKINS, USN
1982 – 1983

CAPTAIN JAMES H. BARTHOLOMEW, USN
1983 -1984

CAPTAIN ROBERT J. TOLLE, USN
1984 - August 1985

REAR ADMIRAL CATHAL L FLYNN, USN
August 1985 - September 1987

REAR ADMIRAL EDWARD "TED" GORDON, USN
September 1988 - Jun 1989

REAR ADMIRAL WILLIAM L. SCHACHTE, JR., USN
June 1989 – 1990

RADM DUVALL M. "MAC" WILLIAMS, JR., USN
October 1990 - October 1992

Senior Civilian SAs titled Deputy Director or Director

Dick Wilson: Feb – May 1966

John "Jack" Lynch: 1966 – until 1976

Earl Richey: 1976 until 1980

Sherm Bliss: 1980-1982

Bert Truxell: 1982-1984

Jack Guedalia: 1984-1986

J. Brian McKee: 1986-1990

Charlie Lannom: 1990-1992

Roy Nedrow: 1992-1997

Dave Brant: 1997-2005

Thomas Betro: 2006- 2009

Mark CLookie: 2010-2013

Andrew Traver: 2013 - 2019

Omar Lopez 2019 -

Accomplishments as seen through the eyes of former NCIS Directors:

[Author's note: *Interviews were conducted years ago of available former Directors; they were asked to discuss memories and mission accomplishments. Many had much to say, so what follows is a small extraction illuminating a small part of their positive memories of their tenure as Director.*]

SA Earl Richey . . . Ability to continue development of a force of professional investigators, begun by my predecessor, SA Jack Lynch, and continued until today. NCIS is rightly considered to be tops in its field.

SA Sherm Bliss . . . The most important case during my tenure was Jonathan Jay Pollard (But with due respect to all, all of the facts have yet to be disclosed. Ron Ruesch and I could add some salient points).

SA Bert Truxell . . . Red Blanket. It was something dictated by the circumstances, but also an operation that would be foreseen as a drain on organizational resources. Those things are easier to get into than to get out of, especially when they are high visibility. The drain did force us to think outside the box regarding the nature / extent of Protective Service Details where the threat subsides but is not eliminated.

SA J. Brian McKee . . . It was the decade of the spy and NCIS performed superbly under the leadership of SAs Palmucci, McCullah, Aldridge, and Worochock. In addition NCIS had a premier Double Agent program which was highly effective and at the forefront within the federal community.

SA Charles Lannom. . . The names of the NCIS during my tenure were: Naval Investigative Service, Naval Security and Investigative Command, Naval Investigative Service Command, and finally Naval Criminal Investigative Service. My biggest challenge . . . to civilianize the overall leadership of NCIS . . .being successful was my proudest accomplishment.

SA Roy Nedrow . . . I would rate the first test of the Cold Case protocol (1994) involving the murder of a Navy officer in the Virgin Islands as one of the most important.

SA Dave Brant . . . NCIS personnel at multiple levels demonstrated the highest moral standards, professional integrity and ethics in their handling of issues concerning interrogation tactics of GTMO detainees.

SA Tom Betro . . . The dedication and sacrifice of the personnel who voluntarily deployed into combat environments to support our men and women in uniform. My inaugural year as Director saw over two hundred deployments to Iraq, Afghanistan, Guantanamo Bay, and the Horn of Africa.

[*Author's Note: While not interviewed in the same time frame as the above Directors, the two comments below are extracted from articles and reflect the thinking of the next two NCIS Directors.*]

SA Mark Clookie: As I depart NCIS, I feel extremely confident in the leadership, our Special Agents and analysts, and our professional staff. They are well trained, dedicated, and committed to protecting Sailors, Marines, and their families and safeguarding Department of the Navy secrets. They have built upon the strong foundation of exceptional dedication and experience of our predecessors.

SA Andrew Traver: The intent of Regional Enforcement Action Capabilities Training (REACT) is to raise the tactical capability of our agents and standardize this capability throughout the Agency. In addition to providing tactical guidance and expertise as needed within on-going investigations, those already trained members of the REACT Team will lead tactical training within their field offices each month.

Chapter 2: **Early History & the Evolution of NCIS**

The Evolution of NCIS
by SA Nick Lutsch

Before February 1966, civilian investigative personnel of our organization worked in something of a gray area. Throughout this period they were part of ONI as little more than a field activity. The majority of them were employed under a confidential contract which could be summarily terminated. If neighbors inquired about the nature of your job, the answer was "research analyst with the Department of the Navy." Investigative personnel had badges and credentials. Weapons were available but generally secured and released only when authorized by a supervisor. The weapons were second-hand as were most of the various vehicles used by the agent personnel. Payday produced what appeared to the rest of the world to be a personal check that was devoid of reference to the actual employer. Consistent with this covert world, investigative personnel did not have their employment records maintained in a typical personnel office. Instead, these records were kept by administrative personnel at each controlling headquarters, co-located with the various world-wide Naval Districts.

Position descriptions were rare. In their place were pay grade statements which, in turn, generally corresponded to the GS grade levels and pay scales. Records physically transferred around the world as personnel relocated and, happily, were rarely lost. On the occasion of an agent's retirement, records needed to be retrieved from various locations and then "processed" at Headquarters prior to being forwarded to a special desk at the Office of Personnel Management. Delays in receiving a retirement payment of any kind from OPM of six months were the norm; some lasted for nearly a year. The agent survived on personal savings until the retirement was approved. In terms of overall agency resources, we were attached like an umbilical cord to the Office of Naval Intelligence; for a host of reasons, that cord was too often unreasonably restricted.

Fortunately, we had some extremely dedicated, far-thinking people at the helm, in particular Jack Lynch and Earl Richey, and, in February 1966, the Naval Investigative Service was established as an echelon 3 organization in the Navy. Though we were still tethered to ONI, we finally had a separate budget line. Resources remained very constrained and organizational issues plagued us for several years thereafter. In the personnel arena, a significant number of our agents continued to work under the "contract" status with all of the adverse implications on their eventual retirement. Another issue was pay for the abnormal hours worked. Regular overtime was not something budgeted for in any serious way. Our fellow agents in other mainstream organizations were drawing pay for Administratively Uncontrollable Overtime (AUO) while NIS special agents more often than not got a pat on the back. In the late 1960's, we were successful in gaining recognition of AUO as a budget item though the funding of it was spotty at best. By way of background, the FBI had AUO incorporated into the standards of OPM in 1954 and agent personnel of that organization routinely received it. In 1969, NIS was finally able to convert its "pay grade" positions into the General Schedule, albeit in the Excepted Service.

This conversion to General Schedule forced a standardization of the position descriptions of the agent cadre of NIS. Standard position descriptions for all grades and all positions were prepared, submitted to OPM and, importantly, certified as law enforcement positions eligible retirement under the provisions of 8336 (c). One immediate benefit of this process was the elimination of the unconscionable delays that had been experienced by agent retirees. All agent positions were established in the 1811 job series and NIS was finally on an equal footing with other law enforcement organizations in the Federal government. Resources remained at critical levels for several years. Regardless, the quest for professionalism across the board had taken hold and was beginning to bear fruit. The issue of good serviceable vehicles was largely resolved through the infusion of about 300 sedans that were surplused early by the Navy Recruiting Command. There was a steady improvement of the facilities of the many field offices of NIS. In direct recognition of the close relationship with the military and our obvious membership in the professional law enforcement community the Navy Federal Credit Union, the United Services Automobile Association (USAA), the Special Agents Mutual Benefit Association (SAMBA) and several other entities opened their doors to NIS / NCIS personnel. These improvement actions and some outstanding investigative and counterintelligence work by NIS were commanding increased focus on our resources.

In November 1985, decisions were made at the Navy Secretariat level to elevate NIS to an Echelon 2 Command with reporting directly to the Secretary of the Navy. This then resulted in the first Flag officer to head NIS, RADM Cathal "Irish" Flynn, and a concurrent decision to physically separate NIS from ONI. In the years following, name changes for the organization went from the Naval Security and Investigative Command (NSIC) to the Naval Investigative Service Command (NISCOM) and finally in 1992 to the name and acronym that is so widely known – the Naval Criminal Investigative Service (NCIS), a professional civilian law enforcement organization within the Department of the Navy.

A TIMELINE

1882: Secretary of the Navy William H. Hunt **established the Office of Naval Intelligence (ONI)** to collect technical information on the world's major naval powers. A subordinate element of ONI would later evolve into today's NCIS. In 1916 **Congress authorized ONI's major expansion to support counterintelligence operations**, which was formalized by Secretary of the Navy James Forrestal in 1945. In addition Secretary Forrestal determined the agency needed civilian investigators for purposes of professional continuity.

1966: The Naval Investigative Service (NIS) was created as a separate entity within ONI with the mission of conducting criminal, counterintelligence, and security background investigations. The new organization answered to the Director of Naval Intelligence (DNI).

1970s: The Special Agent Afloat program began with one agent serving a six month deployment aboard the *USS Intrepid (CV 11)*. In 1977 the Commandant of the Marine Corps began providing **USMC criminal investigators** which enabled the Marine Corps to sustain capability during combat operations.

1980s: NIS began sending agents for training to the **Federal Law Enforcement Training Center (FLETC)**; agents had previously undergone training at NCIS HQ in Suitland, Md. After the bombing of the Marine Corps barracks in Beirut, Lebanon in 1983 NCIS started the **Antiterrorist Alert Center (ATAC).** NCIS was elevated to a full command in 1985, renamed Naval Security and Investigative Command (NSIC) and given the responsibility for the navy's **Information and Personnel Security Program**. In 1988 NSIC Commander Rear Admiral Gordon changed the name to the **Naval Criminal Investigative Service (NCIS)** which remains today.

1990s: In 1992 NCIS was placed under **the direct supervision of the Secretary of the Navy**. In 1993 the **Special Contingency Group** was created to deploy agents in support of operations in major conflict areas. In 1995 the Cold Case Homicide Unit was formed. In 1996 NCIS was **reorganized from a regional structure to a network of field offices reporting directly to NCIS HQ**.

2000s: By an act of Congress, NCIS Special Agents received **authority to arrest civilians and execute federal warrants**. In 2002 the ATAC was reorganized into the **Multiple Threat Alert Center (MTAC)** with the expanded mission to include threats from terrorists, foreign intelligence, criminal, security, and cyber threats. By 2003 NCIS agents were **deploying regularly to Iraq, Afghanistan, and the Horn of Africa**. In 2005 the **Contingency Response Field Office (CRFO)** was created to respond to expeditionary or combat operations. An instruction issued by the Secretary of the Navy in 2005 codified the full functions of NCIS.

ANOTHER BRIEF HISTORY OF NCIS

*[Author's Note: "A Brief History of the Naval Investigative Service" was compiled in 1997 with the conception and approval of NCISHQ staff, but without access to any official sources, investigations, or documents. Therefore, the information therein comes primarily from media sources or memories. The man who compiled this is former NCIS **SA H. Paul Mullis**. He considers that he edited this material; he did not author it. He thanks all who assisted him, with special thanks to **SAs Ron Benefield**, **Gary Comerford**, and **Cole Hanner** from NCISHQ staff. A very small portion of history and memories were extracted and summarized below. Cases were chosen to include to showcase the variety of work and even some humor of the time.]*

In the very early years of what would become ONI and then NIS / NCIS a growing realization occurred to some that the naval community needed to counter spying. Hugely significant was a WWI related incident in 1916 in New Jersey when German saboteurs destroyed a munitions dock, referred to as the "Black Tom" incident. Additionally, networks of Japanese spies were discovered working along the US coastline aboard fishing boats and developing contacts in Japanese-frequented clubs throughout our country. They were collecting information to send back to their homeland before both World Wars. Such activities drove home the need to counter these threats, and through the years following, attention has been focused on how best to prevent such matters costly to our country.

In the early 1900's USMC officer **John Charles Russell** (later Commandant of the Marine Corps) and USN officer and medical doctor **Cecil Coggins** (later to retire as Rear Admiral) helped plan and shape counterintelligence and investigations for the navy In the beginning counterintelligence units were knows as the Naval Secret

Service and agents were known as Secret Service agents. This became a division of ONI.

After the Alger Hiss and Rosenberg's spy cases came to light, understandably background investigations became more important. Those background investigations impacting the Department of the Navy fell to ONI to conduct, which meant heavy caseloads for the mere 150 ONI agents in 1950. Even though the agent corps grew, by 1964 there were 35,000 pending cases, making a six and one-half month backlog for each agent. In 1966 ONI agents became NIS agents, and though criminal investigations were becoming more prevalent, background investigations remained a high priority. In 1972 this task fell away when the Defense Investigative Service (DIS) was formed for the purpose of conducting background investigations. But, with the new agency went half the NIS agents. This left the NIS agent corps at about 500, and it remained relatively stable at that number for many years.

A few of the specific investigations described in the Pullis document are:

- A private investigator hired by an attorney impersonated a USMC Corporal, took up residence on base at El Toro, California for three months and stole files from the legal office to give to the attorney. The man was subsequently arrested by a NIS SA in a local area restaurant, who interrogated the suspect on the spot. The suspect used the tablecloth to draw diagrams of his activities. When leaving the restaurant, the SA purchased the tablecloth to retain as evidence.

- Shortly before deployment someone threw a few large wrenches into the ship's gear, which would prove costly and delay deployment for months. The ship assigned a young officer to assist in interviewing crew members, but after a long investigation it was determined this officer was the perpetrator. His motive was that he married a few days before the ship was to deploy and he wanted more time with his wife. This officer was sentenced to five years in prison and discharged.

- A man who managed a Navy Exchange was suspected of stealing funds since he and his wife had opened numerous new bank accounts. Investigation revealed the couple were simply moving small amounts of their personal money around to new banks, having discovered each time they could acquire a gift of a toaster, coffee pot or the like.

- A USN nurse was raped aboard base in Japan in a darkened room. The perpetrator opened the refrigerator door afterwards to grab a drink, and it was due to this refrigerator light she caught a glimpse of him. The SA used an Identi-Kit to interview victim and construct a drawing. Before the day was out the perpetrator was identified as a man aboard a navy ship. Suspect confessed.

- The United Nations (UN) requested assistance in the interview of a USMC Captain who might have information on an atrocity. The ONI SA assigned to conduct this interview flew from Hawaii to Australia's northernmost point, Point Headland. He got there only to be informed the Captain had moved on to Perth. The agent then flew to Perth. He was then told by the US Consulate the Captain had accepted a position at a mining company in the Great Australian Desert. The ONI agent acquired rental of a Land Rover vehicle and then drove 300 miles the next day to this mining company. Upon arrival the ONI agent found the Captain, interviewed him, got his statement, and then drove back to Perth to return to Hawaii. All-in-all he became known as *"the ONI agent who traveled 25,000 miles to find his man."* Also of note, there was no overtime or compensatory pay in those days.

- A NIS agent relates he was the one and only agent ever assigned to Hong Kong. The office opened in 1967 when Vietnam War military frequently chose to travel to Hong Kong for their rest and recreation (R & R). The same NIS agent closed the office in 1972, but not before he had to move from one home when the rental rate tripled, and then accept a long term rental lease held by the American Consulate. The NIS SA had a one man office which operated out of the Philippines Naval Command spaces. The agent often had to use local drivers for interpreters.

{Authors note: Cecil Coggins, the medical doctor mentioned above, who retired as a Rear Admiral, developed an important operation in his earlier career. What follows is what I wrote based on declassified documents provided to me by SA Vic McPherson. The evolution and methodology of this operation became founded in organizational principles.]

Original naval intelligence reporting of May 15, 1942 (and now declassified) was obtained by NCIS retired SA Vic McPherson. This 20 page report is titled <u>JAPANESE UNDERCOVER ORG – 14th Naval District</u> and was written by Honolulu, Hawaii intelligence

23

officer **C. H. Coggins, LCDR, MC, USN**. This operation was the first successful attempt to recruit widespread sources and reporting within the immigrant Japanese community in the United States, and it established methodology applicable to future operations. This operation was wholly envisioned, crafted and directed by the Naval Intelligence Service on Oahu from July 1941 forward, and was still producing positive results when the report was written at the ten month mark after inception.

LCDR Coggins reflects that six years of prior efforts on the West Coast of the US were largely unsuccessful in recruiting Japanese undercover agents, and laments this was due to various reasons but certainly a big reason was the lack of stressing pro-US vice anti-Japan ideology to potential informants. With the prospect of war looming, agents in Hawaii felt it was imperative to find a way to recruit informants within the Japanese immigrant community. They specifically targeted for recruitment Nisei (second generation Japanese immigrants).

After thorough vetting, agents selected an initial corps group of twelve Nisei. These informants then assisted in recruiting other Nisei, for a final total of 125 informants. Each was assigned a confidential number for reporting purposes. Of these, the first 25 informants were designated the Executive Council and given greater latitude in expansion and control of the operations.

Three months into this operation **agent Joseph P. McCarthy,** who showed great preliminary success, was designated Director and assigned to work the operation full-time. At the ten month mark 985 memorandums had been submitted by informants, each containing information judged to be of great value and each containing between two and six reports.

The operation's success is recounted by LCDR Coggins as due to method of organization, indoctrination and morale, training, and operations:

Method of Organization: Growth of informants was careful. Over 4,000 men were considered by agents as potential informants, and after being checked through military and intelligence agencies, the list was whittled to 400. These 400 names were given to each member of the Executive Council to study and mark only men they considered completely trustworthy and loyal. The results were that 85 men were unanimously recommended by all 25 members of the Executive Council. Thus, these 85 men were recruited to round out the group.

Indoctrination and Morale: Continually stressed to informants was that participation in programs against all enemies of the United States is an essential characteristic of American citizens. Initially each member was given a private weekly meeting to discuss suspects confidentially. After their timidity in reporting in front of others was overcome, they began to discuss matters in open meetings with other informants. It was a process of mutual trust. Intertwined with this was increasing responsibility and much commendation for efforts.

Training: After indoctrination in the necessity for loyalty, hard work, and secrecy, the next step was to train informants in intelligence studies, counterespionage, and undercover work. The Executive Council was trained separately and other members were divided into groups of twenty. Training was held weekly and bi-weekly respectfully. LCDR Coggins lists separate training topics as follows: Interrogations; Surveillance; Pretexts; General Undercover Work; Case Analysis; Report Writing; Analysis of Japanese Clubs and Associations; Analysis of Japanese Religious Sects; Hypothetical and Actual Cases of Espionage; Sabotage and Propaganda; Espionage

Tactics; Modus Operandi of Japanese Espionage (local and national); Modus Operandi of Japanese Espionage (China and Dutch East Indies), Morale Building among local population; Operations of the Sampan Fleet; Japanese Propaganda; and Japanese Psychology and Our Own Propaganda.

Operations: Operational success was judged to be partly due to the combined wealth of knowledge possessed by the informants and to the great variety of professions they represented. An example of the former is - when shown a photograph to the group - within minutes informants identified the man by name, address, and as a former chauffeur for the Japanese Consul who was a procurer of women for the Consul. They also provided his partner's name, sister's name and her place of employment, and his girlfriend's name and her place of employment. Examples of the latter include a CPA who reported on statistical data, an insurance agent who used his position to probe the lives of clients, and a doctor who surveilled other Japanese physicians in possession of Inductotherm apparatus by which they might send radio signals to the enemy. Informants also included an assistant foreman of Japanese stevedores who maintained surveillance over the waterfront, a prominent banker who reported on financial information, and a newspaper reporter who reported on information related to security.

These informants took great pride in their work and provided well-written reports and astute observations and information. They also spent many thousands of man-hours completing special projects. They indexed and translated old copies of Japanese "Who's Who" gathered from attics, translated old newspaper articles originally thought to be innocuous but now considered significant, and indexed Japanese directories. They also made a card index of all adult male Japanese on

Oahu and evaluated each man for patriotic sentiments. As of the report this number was 20,000 and expected to rise to 50,000 men.

In a lengthy but important conclusion, LCDR Coggins writes the work completed by the informants in this operation should serve to encourage similar groups in other Districts, and he highlights rules he considers essential for success:

-Believe and trust in Nisei in order for them to trust you.

-Refer to them as Nisei, not Japanese.

-Maintain personal contacts, keep each member actively employed, and ensure them their efforts are proving their Americanism.

-Remember, enthusiasm is contagious. Recognize and give each man credit for his work.

-Lead - but don't drive or apply pressure of any kind.

-Finally, take a farsighted point of view and remember these men are working for recognition and also for equal opportunities for their children and grandchildren.

Sampling of Memories & Cases Worked prior to 1966

SA Jack Olmstead writes that his early days when he joined ONI in 1962 were a very different world: "JFK was President, Marilyn Monroe died of a drug overdose, a stamp costs 4 cents, and LtCol John Glenn was the first man to orbit Earth. But for SAs in ONI, investigations were far different from those of today. We had non-air conditioned cars, especially fun since we had to wear suits with white long-sleeved shirts. We had a fingerprint kit and lock picks as our "high tech" items. Though we did do some awesome interrogations since Miranda Rights didn't come into play until 1966."

The following is a summary of one case **SA Olmstead** recalls that he solved during interrogation: The Post Office at the Anacostia Naval Yard was burglarized; the crime scene revealed nothing except worthless fingerprints from many who had entered daily. The entrance was a door which had been opened with a screwdriver and hammer; a 'surprise' inspection of sailors' lockers revealed just those tools. The FBI lab identified the screwdriver markings as a definite match. The problem then became that one sailor blamed another and the other blamed the first sailor. During interrogation SA Olmstead was unable to get a confession from either, until he scanned the service record again and noticed the prime suspect had been a Boy Scout. When he reminded the suspect he had not only taken an Oath to the Navy, but also to the Boy Scouts for duty to God and Country, the suspect broke down in tears and confessed. As SA Olmstead notes, "In the days when we agents had little technical means to assist us, we had to get to the truth through careful and crafty investigation. In this case, I had to bring in the Boy Scouts!"

+   +   +   +   +   +

SA Don Mitchell writes about a case he worked in 1961:   He was stationed in Guam from 1959 through 1961. In June 1961 the ONI office in Seattle, Washington contacted ONI in Guam to say there was an arrest warrant from the Seattle PD for one "Leo C. Cardinas" believed to be in Guam. It seems that in 1935 suspect Cardinas got upset with another man in a card game, so he shot and killed him in the lobby of a Seattle hotel. He disposed of the gun, which was later found, fingerprinted, and the prints were sent to the FBI in Washington D.C. Cardinas fled to Alaska to work until he joined the US Navy in 1941. At the time his fingerprints were taken and sent to the FBI there were so many fingerprints coming in the match was missed. Also of note is the Cardinas was not a US citizen.

Suspect Cardinas served in the Navy for the entire war and was honorably discharged in Guam. He married, settled down, and decided to become a US citizen in 1961. He was fingerprinted once again and this time there was a hit. The FBI advised the Seattle PD, who advised the Seattle ONI, who advised Guam ONI. With a warrant in hand for arrest SAs Joe Patton and I found Cardinas at work at Anderson Air Force Base, arrested him, took him back to our office, and interrogated him. Initially he denied involvement but finally confessed and gave a statement.

At a subsequent Guam Federal District Court hearing suspect denied ever knowing me, denied any involvement in the murder, and denied giving me a statement. His wife, standing in the back of the courtroom, yelled that I was a liar, threatened to kill me, and then fainted in a manner that garnered widespread media attention.

Suspect was held in jail in Guam, extradited to Seattle and found guilty of the murder. The judge placed him on probation, and told him to *"leave Seattle, go back to Guam, and find a job to support his wife and eight children. And, stay out of trouble."*

SA Roy Mosteller remembers: I was on a surveillance in San Diego around 1960 with three other agents. The subject under surveillance left a performance at the Old Globe Theater in Balboa Park, and headed for his car parked near the San Diego Zoo. We concluded one of us could take a shortcut through the zoo and view the subject returning to his car. SA Bill Gray took one of our two portable radios and was assisted over the fence. He returned almost immediately, hurtling himself back over the fence with great speed and determination, explaining he had come face to face with a LION. The next day we contacted the zoo to recover our lost radio; it had already been discovered by employees in an enclosure housing a sick lion.

+ + + + + +

By SA Jack Olmstead. In the late 1960s I had to follow-up on a lead with a potential witness in a "peeping-tom" investigation. The potential witness lived in an apartment building in Northeast Washington, D.C. I walked to the door and knocked with the brass knocker, waiting for an answer. A voice from the inside said, "Come in." I tried to keep my voice down a little in the apartment building hallway, and said, "Ma'am, I'm a federal agent. Could you please come to the door?" The voice inside repeated, "Come in." I repeated my statement, adding, I'd rather you come to the door and let me in." The voice said, "Come in" once again . . . and then squawked.

When I realized that I had been talking to a parrot, I sheepishly snuck out of the building and to my car. When I returned to the office at the Washington Navy Yard I made the mistake of telling one of my fellow agents.

My "friends" wrote up requests in my in-box for a background investigation on a *Navy parrot-trooper*, a criminal investigation on a *suspected serial killing parrot*, etc. Fellow agents would leave me messages that a *pirate was on the phone from the Potomac River and was missing his parrot*, and I received a *parrot investigation commendation* from a couple of my buddies.

This incident provided an important lesson - never tell NCIS Special Agents about anything stupid that you ever did!

+ + + + + +

By SA R. Laird Manlove. In 1975, as a boot agent in Memphis, my Supervisor Dick McKenna assigned to me a case in which I was supposed to go do an interrogation of a Naval Reservist up in a rural area of East Tennessee. I called the guy and asked him to meet me at the local sheriff's office in early afternoon. The case involved some complicated pay and allowance issues of getting paid for time not actually worked while the suspect was on active duty in Hawaii.

We met, I warned him and we started talking. He was more than willing to cooperate and began to provide voluminous details about a scam that was ongoing at his command. I developed a lot of cooperation from the guy, and the interrogation was going well.

At four o'clock he asked what time it was and I told him. He said "Mr. Manlove, you told me I could quit talking to you whenever I wanted - didn't you?" I told him that was right, but what was the problem? He said "It's four o'clock! My cows gotta get milked!"

I didn't want to break off the interrogation so we agreed that I should come home with him. We drove high up into the mountains to a small farm on a dirt road and I spent the next couple hours interrogating him while I helped him milk his cows. His wife fixed us dinner, and we spent another few hours at his dinner table writing out a multi-page statement.

It's a good thing I am from a dairy farming family. He told me that a week before, three FBI agents had come to see him about the same thing, but he didn't tell them much. They, apparently, didn't know how to milk cows.

+ + + + + +

By Jack Gelke, CAPT, US Navy (Ret) wrote: "Prior to going on active duty as a ship driver in the Navy, I was a Special Agent with the Office of Naval Intelligence (ONI). I spent three years on the job and was assigned to District Intelligence Headquarters (DIO-6ND), in

Charleston SC I was in my early twenties and single and volunteered to cover investigations throughout our southeast territory, which included a lot of rural and farming areas. This included things like Background Investigations and other types of investigations that might seem tame to the current breed of NCIS agent.

There were a couple of problems with going into the deep woods and rural farms to conduct these investigations. The principal one was the possibility of being mistaken for a *Revenuer,* since white whiskey was a big business in those parts. We had to make it clear to people who could barely read or write that our credentials showed us to be those of Special Agents of the US Navy and not the dreaded Alcohol and Tobacco Tax Agents - it wasn't easy and we never showed a badge!

The other type of investigations was *fraud* investigations, involving secondary allotments for sailor's and marine's relatives. These dependents had to have limited incomes. We had to verify that farming and other incomes met the parameters of the law. As a result I became quite an expert, with help from the local County Agent, in the price yields of all types of produce and farm animals (including pigs, chickens, and eggs) and also *cash* crops such as tobacco, so I could estimate their farm incomes. The most unusual situation I had during one of these investigations involved surprising a relative in the home - sewing baseballs! She got $.50 apiece for sewing them, which I had to duly note as income in my report."

By SA George Reis. "I spent several days investigating a series of arsons at the Naval Training Center, San Diego (NTCSD). Most of the fires were minor in nature, usually trash containers, but then the arsonist began getting more serious and attempted a fire under the base acetylene tank storage. Finally, his last attempt consisted of putting a timed ignition device on the seat of an abandoned pick up truck, which he parked over the bases fuel tanks, but this fizzled out. (The device was a cigarette, placed in a match book next to a baggie of gasoline. The cigarette was supposed to burn down to the matches, which would ignite with a flash and cause the gasoline baggy to explode in fire. Well, the cigarette fizzled out, and no ignition took place, but now I had his M.O.)

About a week later the Base Security advised us that a sailor had gone UA (Unauthorized Absence), and their search of his locker disclosed two bleach bottles filled with gasoline, a multitude of match books, and baggies. Shore Patrol in Los Angeles, CA apprehended him, and delivered him to the NTC holding cell, and I was called in the middle of the night to interrogate him. After a body search for weapons or items of interest to the Arson, the giggling sailor was found to have many matchbooks in the lining of his leather jacket. He was then taken by me to my small interrogation room, just above the Commandant's office in the NTC Commandant's Center.

After a Miranda warning, my approach was to be complimentary of his ingenuity, and I asked him, "When did you set your first fire?" Proudly he told me it was when he set fire, and severely burned, his baby brother. He then told me of other fires he had set, which extremely pleased him, and he admitted to setting fires on the NTC. He said he would take me to the rooftops of many barracks buildings, where he stored his gasoline in bleach bottles. Then I asked him what his next intended target was, and he said right where we are sitting. "It is the Commandant's office," he said, "and I want to get him, and this whole building."

The next day the base Fire Marshal, happy with my results, went with me to brief the Commandant. I advised that I had found the culprit and he had confessed. The Commandant responded in an angry manner, saying, "*What took you so long?*" It was then that I told him that he and his office were the next target of the arsonist. That ended the discussion with the Commandant!

My conclusion was that a pyromaniac was out of commission, and I personally felt better."

[Author's note: **SA George Reis** *was also a talented portrait artist, who often shared his artwork within NCIS. I chose two of my favorites to include in this book. The first is a portrait of his mother and the second is a self-portrait.]*

George Reis' mother

SA George Reis

... and a few more cases worked shortly after 1966

SA Lance Arnold remembers conducting interviews on cases while assigned to Charleston, West Virginia circa 1968 Some of these took him into *backwoodsy* areas, such as this interview:

Location was Viper, Harlan County, Kentucky – As we approached the target old house, way back in the hills, to seek corroboration, an elderly gentleman exited as we entered the dirt driveway . We immediately observed that the man had a pistol on his side; we were probably armed with the standard issue S&W 357 Magnum. These leads were approached with substantial apprehension, partly due to our inexperience but also, the sensitive nature of the case and civilian status of the interviewee . But, we proceeded, and after several minutes of exchange of pleasantries and assurance we were no threat to him and emphasis on National Security, we conducted a brief interview. I might point out that we were dressed in coat and tie, and driving an obvious government vehicle . As I recall, he denied the allegations, and don't recall many interrogations tricks! Policy required negative statements at the time . The old Royal portable typewriter was placed on the hood of the car, and a brief statement of denial prepared . When asked to read and sign the document, he stated he never learned to read or write . He was requested to make his "X" and witnessed by participating agents . He was a friendly old gentleman and explained he did not go to school much because his father had assassinated the governor of Kentucky and was in prison . (true or not – don't know) When asked about his weapon, he said he was going to the barn to shoot rats. Again, don't know, but we got the hell out of there.

+ + + + + +

SA George McClellan sent in the following information regarding his career (focused on his memories of his earliest days): I started as a contract agent in 1969, which meant I signed a yearly contract, renewable every year unless I went afoul. A month after I was hired NIS changed to "excepted civil service." I was a GS-7 step 5. I started in the Los Angeles area with SA Chuck Hurley as my Supervisor, and I was employed by NIS for four years before I went to the Agents Basic School. I retired as a GS-13 in 1990; my last office was at the Naval Air Station Atlanta in Marietta, Georgia.

In the beginning I was shocked to learn NIS agents dressed like FBI agents, with suits, white shirts and ties and, an eastern favorite, fedora's (felt hats). Comfortable Wing Tipped shoes were almost a uniform requirement too. No one was ever allowed to wear other than the prescribed professional ensemble. Southern California was too hot to wear a hat so most agents there, except one or two raised on the east coast, never wore one but always had one nearby in case the Supervising Agent came through on an inspection or by accident.

In late 1970, we got a new Supervising Agent in NCIS San Diego, in the person of Mr. Sherm Bliss. He came with a tough reputation for being a hard NIS man with all its trappings. Then, he made his grand tour of the offices in the 9th Naval District. We were at Norton Air Force Base then. We awaited his arrival with fearful anticipation and lo, he shows up wearing a beautiful grey silk suit, blue shirt, I say it again, BLUE Shirt with silk tie, and his coat thrown over his arm. After introductions and a short chat, he wanted to know if it was too early to visit the Officers Club for a libation. What a character he was; white shirts immediately disappeared forever.

Our issued credentials were two 3x5 printed cards in a thin leather case that fit comfortably in the shirt pocket. They were held there by a spring steel clip. When I did my three hour employment interview, I ask the Supervising Agent, Mr. Earl Richie, why the clip - and he said ... *"if you lose your box tops, you can walk west until your hat floats."* Understood!

In the 60's and 70's, we were a "beggar" organization. Our cars were cheap, old, and without air conditioning. Then a miracle happened. Mr. Bliss had to drive through the desert. All the clothing in his suitcase was ruined by the extreme heat when toiletries burst or leaked. He nearly fainted from exhaustion driving in this oven of a car. In short order every "desert" NCIS station got a call to drive our old cars to San Diego and collect new 1972 air conditioned Ford cars with V8 engines. The result: SA Sherm Bliss was the most popular agent ever!

We had a badge but it was small, heavy and mounted in a wrap around, snap closed leather case to be carried secretly in the pants pocket attached to a watch chain. We were forbidden to tell people we were Special Agents of Naval Intelligence or the Naval Investigative Service. We couldn't even tell our friends and neighbors. We could only say we were Federal Agents.

\+ + + + + +

Humorous Take on Agents' Vocabulary (back in the day)

-**RELIABLE SOURCE:** The guy you just met.
-**DEVELOPED INFORMANT:** The guy who told the guy you just met.
-**UNIMPEACHABLE SOURCE:** The guy who originally started the rumor.

-**IT IS IN THE PROCESS:** So wrapped in red tape the situation is hopeless.
-**UNDER CONSIDERATION:** Never heard of it.
-**UNDER ACTIVE CONSIDERATION:** We are looking in the files for it.
-**WE WILL LOOK INTO IT**: By the time the wheel makes a full turn, we assume you will have forgotten about it.
-**WE ARE CHECKING THE FILES**: We need more time to think of an answer.

-**COORDINATOR**: One whose desk is between two expeditors.
-**CONSULTANT** (or expert): Any ordinary guy more than 50 miles away from home.
-**NOTE AND INITIAL**: Let's spread the responsibility for this.

\+ + + + + +

Birth of NIS - leading to the Modern NCIS

Born from within the Office of Naval Intelligence (ONI) the Naval Investigative Service (NIS) was established February 4, 1966. NIS changed names a few times in later years, and expanded in mission, but NIS is essentially the organization known today as NCIS. Thus, NCIS celebrated the year 2016 as the organization's 50th birthday. Establishment of NCIS was via <u>Secretary of the Navy Notice 5150</u> of February 4, 1966. The subject is Naval Investigative Service, establishment of.

SA Blair Gluba provided information regarding the naming of NIS: In a 1965 Department of Defense (DoD) study it was recommended that there be a separate investigative service in the Department of the Navy. SAs Jack Lynch, Dick Wilson and Sherm Bliss came up with the name during an afternoon office discussion.

SA Jack Lynch contributed the word *investigative*, noting the title should reflect the mission directive. **SA Sherm Bliss** contributed *Naval* vice Navy to recognize inclusion of the Marine Corps, and **SA Dick Wilson** contributed the word *service* noting that naval intelligence itself had once been known as a service. Thus was born the title **Naval Investigative Service.**

Organizational lore embraces **SA Charles "Dick" Wilson** as *Mr. ONI*. Fittingly, SA Wilson retired on April 30, 1966, just a few months after elements of ONI became NIS. SA Wilson retired with over 30 years of federal service; 20 of these were as a SA for ONI. In his honor a huge party was thrown at the Naval Officers' Club Bethesda, Maryland. Many Admirals and senior civilians were in attendance.

SA John "Jack" Lynch became entrenched in the new organizational lore as *Mr. NIS*. The following remarks are from **SA Allen Carballo,** the son-in-law of SA Jack Lynch: "Jack served with ONI from November 1954 until his retirement in 1976. Jack was described to him as the "Father of NIS" because he was one of the early architects that built the foundation supporting what NCIS is today. Jack was also a naval officer who served from 1933-1954. His active naval service included assignments aboard WWII warships - where he received a Purple Heart - and an assignment during the Korean War where he served aboard an aircraft carrier."

SA George Reis writes on ONI becoming NIS in Vietnam: "When the organization changed in name and mission in 1966, agents were already working in the combat area of Vietnam. **SA Bob Kain** was the first ONI agent permanently assigned as Resident Agent in Saigon. His replacement was **SA Maynard Anderson**, who was later joined by **SAs Tom Brannon**, **Milt Steffen** and **Paul Carr** in early 1965. With the establishment of NIS, Naval Investigative Service Office (NISO) Vietnam stood up in April 1966. **LCDR William Manthorpe** was the first NISO Vietnam CO, and **SA Ken Nickel** was the first Supervising Agent. In-country tours were voluntary only and set at one year, which was the same duration for all military."

Chapter 3: **VIETNAM**

NCIS agents were in-country Vietnam in support of naval operations. The agent tours were voluntary and for one year; some volunteered for more. The camaraderie among the agents who worked in Vietnam has stood the test of time. Regularly scheduled Vietnam agent reunions are well attended events of former NCIS agents.

SA Doug Hubbard spent a total of 36 months in Vietnam and has written a book about his experience. He has generously shared information with NCISA; here is one background extract:

"During the thirteen-year period in which ONI/NIS Agents were deployed to the Republic of Vietnam, the in-country Agent force never exceeded twenty men. Of the twenty, three were supervisory personnel: a Supervising Agent, and two Senior Resident Agents overseeing offices in Saigon and DaNang with their distant one-Agent satellite units. At the 1969 peak US war commitment, 550,000 troops were in-country, with Navy and Marine Corps components concentrated in the far north and southern Mekong Delta regions.

The NISO Vietnam Agent force was made up entirely of volunteers drawn from across the global spectrum of NIS field offices. All had agreed to serve a minimum of twelve months in an active war zone. Married Agents knew that they would not see their wives and children during their tour of duty, excepting a five-day R&R typically spent in

Honolulu. Internet did not exist, fax machines had yet to be invented and long-distance phone connections were unavailable. US Mail was the only tie to "The World". Agent volunteers were a diverse group, motivated to serve by many factors: potential early promotion to journeyman Agent status, preferred duty station assignment post tour, a spirit of adventure, increased salaries – and there were personal reasons which typically later presented themselves in the often-cloistered Vietnam environment.

Agents arrived in Vietnam without special training or equipment excepting their issue Smith and Wesson Model 19 .357 Combat Magnum and copy of the ONI 63-1B Manual for Investigations which typically arrived at their new duty station soon after they did by Registered US Mail. Many volunteers had never conducted a criminal investigation. All of us were soon indoctrinated into an environment characterized by an abundance of violent crime in a particularly brutal war. I spent 36 months at NISO Vietnam; I was also the youngest Special Agent to serve. There is a long list of older Agents to whom I owe my success in that unique and dangerous environment, men who patiently guided and mentored me – and I am certain all who served owe much to others who took time to help with a very steep learning curve. Hence, the Agent clan was tightly knit then, and it remains so. Our reunions are ample proof of the unique ties developed during what many remember as the most intense year of their lives."

The following are excerpts from an article on Vietnam written by **SA Jack Donnelly** in 1966:   Weather is sunny and hot or damp depending on the time of year   -   streets are full of people and bicycles, as for working hours the saying on Fridays "Just two more working days until Monday". -   Cases are criminal, security /

subversive and counterintelligence functions. - Travel is an occasional trip to Bangkok or Hong Kong, but mostly places such as Can Tho, Pleiku, Chu Lai, etc. - Incidents include three agents and the OIC in two cars stoned by a group of restless youths; two different agents that were spit upon; one agent checking into the Army BOQ at Can Tho who was given a room key and a towel, along with a thorough brief on the fields of fire he was to maintain in the event the Viet Cong attacked – all guests were given this brief which presented an interlocking, impassable barrier for an attackers!

+ + + + + +

SA Todd Hannah remembers this case: In January 1968 I was transferred to the office at Subic Bay. Shortly after arrival, I was assigned a narcotics investigation aboard the aircraft carrier *USS Bon Homme Richard (CV-31),* which was enroute from Hawaii to the Philippines. When it arrived, the initial informant (also guilty) implicated a few others, but the case seemed resolved prior to the ship's sailing for "Yankee Station" off the coast of North Vietnam. Not so, because shortly we received a message from the ship: An offender wanted to implicate others in exchange for release from the brig.

I was flown to the ship by way of Danang, Republic of Vietnam where I spent one night before proceeding to "Yankee Station". The Danang Resident Agency had quarters in a two story cement villa surrounded by a wall. I was awakened in the middle of the night by the sound of automatic rifle fire outside and heard bare feet hitting the floor and running around upstairs. Since I was "new to the area," I felt it would be prudent to go upstairs and find out what the excitement was about. When I reached the top of the stairs, I had to bust out laughing at the site of men in their skivvies wearing only flak jackets and helmets armed with their automatic weapons and crouching behind a three foot wall overlooking the front of the house. It turned out the gun fire was caused by mistaken identities between two Vietnamese police officers.

The next day, I was flown out to the ship. Anyone who has had the experience approaching a carrier by plane will agree how tiny that ship looks in such a big ocean. The thought of landing on it sent a chill up my spine, but we landed without any trouble. The sailor who wanted out of the brig generated more names to be investigated. Eventually, the case expanded to include 94 sailors, but only two or three of them were what I considered hard core pushers that would eventually face a General Court Martial.

I was escorting one of these "pushers" plus a stack of documented confessions on one of my return trips. As bad as it was landing on the carrier, it was not a comfortable feeling knowing that one of the people involved was assigned to determine when the catapult pressure was sufficient for our take off! (FYI: The case had leads extending back to the US and to Mexico.)

+ + + + + +

SA Tom Brannon, assigned to DaNang, Republic of Vietnam on October 17, 1965 advised he was able to establish a permanent ONI office in one week. He provided a copy of a Letter of Appreciation he received for his work, which states: "During the period October 17, 1965 through February 5, 1966 you have brought more than forty cases to a successful conclusion. Your support of the III Marine Amphibious Force has been exemplary. The record and reputation you left behind are evidence of the high personal standards you maintain and of your devotion to your profession."

+ + + + + +

SA Tom Brannon also writes about the bombing of the US Embassy on March 31, 1965: **SA Maynard Anderson** decided to visit the Embassy in downtown Saigon and asked me to accompany him. Minutes prior to arriving we heard an explosion; we arrived to find the Viet Cong had placed C-4 plastic explosive in an old French automobile and parked it in front of the embassy. The explosion killed 17 people and wounded 151 others, including 45 Americans. I was near the main door when I saw wounded US Ambassador Alex Johnson leave in the company of a US Marine security guard.

TET OFFENSIVE

[Author's Note: In late January 1968, during the lunar New Year (or Tet) holiday, North Vietnamese and communist Viet Cong forces launched a coordinated attack against a number of targets in South Vietnam. The US and South Vietnamese militaries sustained heavy losses before finally repelling the communist assault. This was the first phase, and one referred to in this article. The other two phases were conducted in late spring and late summer of the same year.]

NIS agents in Saigon during the January 31, 1968 TET Offensive (Vietnamese New Year Attack) were interviewed by JO2 Darlene Jensen for an article. The following are excerpts from that article:

SA Fred Seehorn was in charge at the Saigon office. He discussed this Viet Cong (VC) attack, which came at a time when defensive forces were thin. It was the civilian SAs who had to gather together in their command. They became the first NIS personnel to defend their command against hostile forces.

SA Bob Tugwell says issues NIS agents working in Saigon faced everyday were "a million people going every which way on foot, bicycles, motor cycles, Pedi cabs, . . . traffic was unimaginable . . . like nothing one can imagine . . . in order to relieve themselves men, women, children, and animals just went in the streets . . . 10 feet high piles of garbage were in the streets . . . tin and cardboard shacks were everywhere. "

Transportation meant hitching a ride on a helicopter, linking up with a convoy or riverboat, or holding up a sign reading "Saigon". **SA Larry Ferrell** remembers that **SA Don Webb** arranged transportation one day and they ended up in the back of a vegetable truck following a convoy! **SA Tom Ferguson** says there weren't enough cars to go around for dating, dining, or going to a bar, so he didn't get out often. After the TET Offensive no one got out for entertainment at all.

NCIS office Saigon was located in the COFAT compound Cholan/Saigon or Chinese sector. A former wealthy home was converted to government use, and an 8' high wall was built all around, along with an Iron Gate and door. There were sand bags around and a Vietnamese guard 24 hours a day.

SA Darden Nelms recalls the day of the attack as being sunny and quiet. "At 0730 I noticed an armored personnel carrier in front of the gate to the compound, I remember a rifle crack and somebody saying. - We are under attack". At some point heard over a radio transmission was "They have hit the compound – they have got it – they have over-run COFAT compound." Listening to radio transmissions NIS agents could hear the VC getting closer, the gun fire, the MPs asking for permission to use their grenade launchers, etc.

An Army officer came running in and said "We have secured the Explosive Ordinance Disposal. You are responsible for this sector" What? **SA Tugwell s**aid at the time he thought of a few firefights he had been close to, but it never occurred to him he could get hurt; he was more concerned about getting lost in the jungle when traveling to work cases. **SA Seehorn** said he remembers wondering how long they were going to have to stay in the compound because at first he thought it was a small ambush and would be over quickly.

SA Seehorn said it got quiet, and there was no doubt that the Vietnamese and Chinese knew what was happening because the streets became suddenly deserted of those usually going to market and such. **SA Seehorn** continues "As the Viet Cong got closer we heard them and saw them . . . People were running, screaming, shooting . . . Bullets were hitting the wall and ricochets set the grass, trees and shrubs on fire. Our next concern was for our classified material, but we decided we didn't have anything highly classified enough to get people killed over."

At one point Viet Cong surrounded the compound and some got into an area behind the office spaces. All communication was cut off. Military representative LCdr William Bruebaker told us we couldn't properly defend the compound. **SA Bill Ward** went to his good friend at the nearby Air Force Office of Special Investigations (OSI) and came back with borrowed M-16s, M-1s, and whatever automatic weapons he could get his hands on. **SA Seehorn,** having formerly been in the Army, tried to provide us with instant training on how to hold and fire these weapons.

The NIS agents, spaced about every 5 to 10 feet, manned the walls. **SA Ward** said they were on duty 24 hours a day on two hour shifts, for about three or four days. They slept on the floor when they could. After several days they made it from the office back to their BOQ rooms which were more heavily protected.

None will ever forget their shared experience of this time.

+ + + + + +

SA Carl Merritt writes: The NIS Vietnam experience began in 1962 and was initially limited to individual Special Agents, being dispatched for temporary duty, from the ONI office in the Philippines. The first agent was Bob Kain; other early agents are shown below:

The first ONI Special Agents and ONI 9592 Agents assigned to Vietnam (c. 1962-3) (L-R) Agent Mord Tucker, SA Maynard Anderson, Agent Sam Houston, SA Bob Kain, LT Leroy Hayden, USN (Photo credit Sam Houston, pictured above)

+ + + + + +

2010 VIETNAM REUNION: A plaque containing the names of all of the Commanding Officers of NCIS Vietnam and all of the civilian NCIS Special Agents who served in Vietnam was presented to NCIS Director **SA Mark Clookie** by NCISA President (and Vietnam veteran) **SA Bob Powers**. The Plaque was the idea of **SA John Dill IV** who designed it and had it engraved.

Chapter 4: **NCIS Expansions Employees / Methodology**

NCIS Reserve Special Agents

In a 1991 article written by **Commander Stan Brooks**, NCIS Reserve Coordinator, he discusses the history of naval reserve support to NCIS. He relates that in the 1920s reserve agent units were formed to support ONI. During WWII the majority of intelligence officers in the navy were reservists.

Commander Brooks writes of the importance of fully trained and mobilization-ready reservists, and discusses recent restructuring in billets and in training to provide a higher level of support from reservists to NCIS.

What follows are extracts of an article submitted by Reserve NCIS **SA Jay Caputo** about 5 years ago. At the time he was Chief of Detectives of the Nassau County NY Police Department. Also, he was a Captain in the naval reserves. In this article he notes after 9/11 his NCIS reserve unit out of Newport *"was mobilized and we all were sent far and wide to such places as Bahrain, Iceland, London, Naples, Rota, with a few intrepid souls venturing in country in Iraq."*

Captain Caputo mentions what many reservists brought to NCIS:

CAPT Drew Lieb worked his way up from a Detective in the New Jersey State Police to Lt Col in charge of counter-terrorism for the agency, and finally as Deputy Director for the NJ Department of Homeland Security. He deployed with NCIS to the Middle East where his bomb training was put to use many times.

CDR Bill Seidenstein served in Bahrain and Naples during Operation Desert Storm. He brought with him tremendous skills from his job as Commander of NYPDs Kings County (Brooklyn) District Attorney's squad.

CDR Jack McKeon served with Rockville Centre PD on Long Island NY for over 37 years, rising up through investigations to become the Police Commissioner. His service with NCIS included locations all over New England to include NCISHQ.

Others include: **CAPT Manny Ortega** who was an Inspector with New Bedford, Mass PD. **CDR Pat Shanley** who worked for the PD in Wallingford, CT. **LCDR Bob Ferguson** who was a Captain with the NJ State Police. **CDR Pete Lovecchio** who worked for San Jose PD in CA. **CAPT Pat Gildea** who was a Captain with Huntington Beach PD in CA. **ISC Robert Tanaglia** who worked for Massachusetts Department of Corrections. **LT Michael Gagne**r who was a Sergeant with the Fairfield CT PD. **ENS Ed Ramos** who was a Detective with the Springfield Massachusettes PD and then became a NCIS SA full time. **CDR Tom Keating** who was a Ranger with the National Park Service. **CDR Mike Alonge** who was a Nassau County Court Judge. **CDR David Chiaro** who was a Nassau County Highway Patrol officer. **CAPT Dave Perry** who was an investigator with the FBI.

+ + + + + +

SA Bill Holt was a USNR NCIS officer agent who recalled his first drill weekend in 1988. "I was assigned as part of an honor guard at the gravesite of a retired Navy Captain. Standing by the open grave at 'attention' I managed to lock my knees and cut off the blood to my brain. I fell backwards into the funeral flowers and then pitched forward into the grave, saved only by the other honor guard members." Following this incident I "served with distinction as the unit donut officer and urinalysis officer". He went on to say, "But then I served with many great professional folks at NCIS New London and NCIS Newport to include time in London and Iceland."

SA John R. "Randy" Carter wrote an article about his time with the NCIS Reserve agents beginning in 1983. At the time he was a Special Agent with the US Customs Service in Jacksonville, Florida. His first NCIS case was working a fraud complaint, along with **SA Dale Wallace,** at NAS Jacksonville. His next active duty was in support of a PSD regarding the visit of the British Sea Lord to the King's Bay Submarine Base in Southeast Georgia. [*Author's note: The professional head of the British navy is an Admiral titled First Sea Lord.]* **SA Carter** said there were concerns due to a scheduled Green Peace demonstration at the front gate of the base, so he suggested an alternative to a limo ride through there: Use a bus and enter through a back gate. The Sea Lord's response "I have never ridden on an American school bus and I look forward to it!"

Upon retirement from his civilian job in 2000, **SA Carter** was mobilized for a two year assignment at NCIS Guantanamo Bay to help with logistics and cases. He was able to quickly secure vehicles for use, and to secure a boat for use by the office. He did this through an interagency transfer from Customs to NCIS. The boat was a vessel seized in a drug interdiction, and SA Carter describes it as: A 27' Fountain, center console with blue lights, Loran, GPS, with twin 200

Mercury engines. He also notes that while there he participated in interrogations of Al' Qaeda detainees. From his tour there he went to the Counterintelligence Task Force (CITF) at Ft. Belvoir as the assistant SA in charge for the Preliminary Investigations Branch. After that tour he worked as a training instructor at FLETC.

USMC CID / NCIS   Special Agents

A 1999 article titled <u>Marine, Navy Criminal Units Merge</u> written by Stephanie Cain for the Marine Corps Times states that on May 18, 1999 the Marine Corps' Criminal Investigative Division (CID) merged with the Naval Criminal Investigative Service (NCIS). This merger was approved by **NCIS Director David Brant** and **LtGen Martin Steele**, USMC Deputy Chief of Staff for Plans, Policies, and Operations.

Sharing resources is nothing new; beginning in 1976 a cadre of investigators from the USMC CID have undertaken three to five year tours with NCIS.   With this merger the current number of Marines working with NCIS as Special Agents will increase from 40 to 75. Those who haven't already received training in felony investigations will do so.

In terms of NCIS, gains outlined from this merger include the fact that the USMC will retain funding for training, transfers, and salaries for CID agents, but they will assist NCIS in filling personnel needs for a growing NCIS mission. Also, inclusion of more USMC CID agents brings a different and valuable perspective that helps NCIS better understand commanders' concerns. According to Director Brant "It sets the stage for developing and exercising new and better doctrine to bring the full weight of NCIS capability to bear in support of the Marine mission."

+   +   +   +   +   +

In an article written in 1996 by **SA Ken Oglesbee,** he describes the life and career of a Marine CID agent assigned to NCIS. This man is **Staff Sergeant Brian Jackson**, who works with NCIS El Toro, California where SA Oglesbee is the supervisor. Summary follows:

SSgt Jackson grew up on the mean streets of Los Angeles County, but through hard work and tough choices he beat the odds. He is working with NCIS and nearly finished with his college degree with plans to go on to law school. That said, he didn't forget his family or his roots. A younger brother and sister attend the same rough elementary school he attended. He mentors his young siblings and has visited this elementary school to relate his experiences and choices to classrooms full of young children.

+ + + + + +

In 1966 **SA Larry Fuentes** began his career on active duty as a USMC tank driver, which included tours in Vietnam. He later became a USMC CID agent, and in 1980 he continued as a USMC reservist,

but became a civilian NCIS Special Agent. As a Marine Corps reservist he achieved the rank of Chief Warrant Officer 4 before retiring. He served more than 30 years as a civilian NCIS Special Agent. During these years he readily volunteered for many challenging jobs, including a tour in Iraq.

Special Agent Fuentes finished his career as an instructor at the Federal Law Enforcement Training Center.

+ + + + + +

SA Patrick Hickson submitted the following: "I entered the US Marine Corps in June 1975 with a desire to become a military policeman (MP), but found myself being a cannoneer instead. Nevertheless, I pursued my desire, received a temporary transfer to be an MP, and this was followed by a permanent position in 1979.

In 1982 I received a transfer to Cherry Pt., North Carolina to work as a military special agent with NCIS, and was transferred two years later to Okinawa, Japan to work in the same capacity.

I attended night school to earn my college degree, which gave me the education I needed for a civilian NCIS Special Agent position. I transferred from active duty to a reservist in the Marine Corps in 1987, the year I was hired and began a civilian career with NCIS as an agent. I retired in 2009 after more than 20 years in this job.

My career included Special Agent Afloat tours on both the *USS Independence (CV-62)* and the *USS Nimitz (CV-68),* along with many other locations, including NCIS Headquarters."

Female NCIS Special Agents

Females were not hired as civilian NCIS Special Agents until the 1970s. It is impossible to know the totality of consideration given to hiring female ONI / NCIS agents through the years, but what follows is a clue of the discussion on two occasions. **SA Vic McPherson,** while searching archived material, sent me copies of some memorandums he discovered on this subject. Originally bearing a *confidential* classification, these documents were declassified on September 2, 1978. The discussion was whether or not to hire female agents; the conclusion was a definite **NO**.

A lengthy memorandum dated October 6, 1950, titled *ONI Operatives; Employment of Women as,* was written and signed by **T.J. Mullikin**, addressed to **USN Captain E. P. Hylant**, and sent via **Mr. C.R Wilson**. At this time Mullikin and Wilson were ONI agents and Captain Hylant was, presumably, a senior officer in the ONI chain of command.

Mullikin writes a two page memo expressing his opinion, and in doing so, crafts together a series of female stereotypical gender characteristics that are incomprehensible in today's world. He states the only type of investigation a female agent should be considered for is investigation of lesbians (homosexuals were not allowed in military service during this time), but he concludes this is not a good idea. Why? Because, he says, an operative "is essentially a masculine occupation. Certain characteristics essential to a successful operative are lacking in the normal feminine type. Characteristics typifying masculinity will be found in most women willing to be operatives, but . . . those who would stay with such an assignment would very probably be at least latent lesbians with a sublimation of sadistic expression, such as coming from the detection and prosecution of lesbians."

Mullikin writes if women are employed to work on lesbian cases, insurmountable difficulties would arise. He says women can confess many things to men, but "find it extremely difficult to confess their shortcomings to other women. A lesbian of the feminine type will not debase herself before another woman. . . . A lesbian of the masculine type has a deep and abiding contempt for other women except as sexual instruments . . . "

In terms of general investigative work, Mullikin goes on to dismiss women's ability to interrogate suspects by writing "not more than one male operative in twenty can be called a really good interrogator. Master interrogators cannot be developed. It is a talent which combines sensitivity toward other people, vast patience, a photographic memory for details of conversation, practical psychology and experience. The chances of obtaining women who are entirely normal and who overcome their natural repugnance for the assignment and who moreover were good interrogators are very remote."

In a handwritten notation Mr. Wilson writes on the bottom of this memorandum: "Concur strongly in these observations. Believe the employment of female operatives would achieve no practical success whatsoever." He initials his comments, fulfilling his "via" role in this memorandum.

Obviously the issue of hiring female agents arose again a few years later. There is another memorandum, from **Captain Hylant** to

Admiral Espe dated October 9, but with no year written. In this memorandum **Captain Hylant** attaches the memorandum summarized above and states "I concur with the observations and beliefs of Mr. Mullikin and recommend that we do not employ females in this special field." **Rear Admiral Carl F. Espe** served as the Director of Naval Intelligence from December 1952 to May 1956, so it is most likely within these years that this issue was revisited.

These are neither insignificant documents nor views of unimportant people in NCIS history. As written earlier, Mr. C. R. "Dick" Wilson is much acclaimed and often referred to in the lore of early NCIS as *Mr. ONI.*

SA Mullikin doesn't write what credentials he has to come to his conclusion about the inability of females to conduct interrogations. That claim was proven untrue by the first female civilian agent hired by NCIS. She became a respected polygrapher known for her superb interrogation skills.

That first civilian female agent was **SA Debbie Baughman**, who was previously a US Marine Corps officer. She and four other women were hired in 1977-1978 as agents. They were **SA Diana Collins**, who became the first female agent to be assigned aboard an aircraft carrier, SA **Marya Gripp**, **SA Renea King**, and **SA Tricia Mansell** (author), who became the first female agent to be assigned to a supervisory position at NCIS HQ in Washington DC.

Other early female SAs were **Angelic White, JoAnn Yutronich, Kim Myers, Julie Herrmann, Bernie Ayres, Joan Barron,** and **Roni McCarthy,** among others, hired within the next few years..

Of particular interest is that **SAs Angelic White** was the first woman hired as a Special Agent who was the daughter of a NCIS agent. There were a number of father-son agents, but on May 11, 1981, she became the first ever daughter agent. Her father was **SA Stan White**

Secretaries & Analysts

[Author's note: Upon reflecting on the information contained in the first draft of this book, it was clear to me that most people mentioned were male and special agents. I believe there are three reasons for this: 1) In the early days there were only agents and secretaries in the organization; secretaries rarely contributed memoirs to historical documents, and all agents were male. 2) The NCIS organization didn't widen to include female agents until the 1970s, and analytical positions until the 1980s. This book contains many memories that pre-date that timeframe. 3) For whatever reason, few female agents or analysts have written historical accounts of their earlier years with NCIS.]

I feel compelled to say a few words about the contributions of these people. When I was hired and first worked at NCIS North Island, there were about a dozen agents and two or three secretaries. The two secretaries I remember most are **Joy Petty** and **Susan Rose**. In my opinion they were critical to daily business. In those days agents had neither typewriters or computers at their disposal; all investigative matters were dictated by agents and then given to secretaries to transcribe and type.

Joy Petty was the senior secretary in this office. Her years of knowledge about so many things effecting the base commands and the carriers in port was vast. Agents came and went, but many times, issues were cyclical. Joy's contribution to the smooth running of this office was invaluable.

Susan Rose came to NCIS North Island as a young, bright, enthusiastic secretary. I have no idea how she acquired the job, but

NCIS was a big winner with her employment. After a few years at this office, Susan left to transfer to NCIS Headquarters. She had become someone on the ground floor of the computer age, quickly learning hardware and software issues. From headquarters she traveled widely to assist in installing computer systems in many NCIS offices.

I still consider both of these hardworking, bright, intelligent, and wonderfully kind ladies to be great friends.

My first time working with analysts was at NCIS Headquarters in the 1980s, and I remember most **Watson Pryor** and **Suzanne Henderson.** Watson worked in the same office I worked in, which was the office supervising double agent operations. Watson's duties were to handle certain types of information collection, conduct research, and produce informative documents. His mere presence in the office added to our cheerful camaraderie, because he was such a nice man.

Suzanne worked with the anti-terrorism alert center, and like most analysts there, was assigned a geographical area of expertise. Years later, when I worked in Hawaii, Suzanne came out for many weeks to assist me. I appreciated her work ethic and her knowledge, and realized the great extent that she contributed to NCIS.

There are many other secretaries and analysts I worked with, but since space here is limited, let me just mention one more in detail: *Little Tricia.* In the small office at NCIS Headquarters there weren't many people, but I worked in this office along with a young secretary named Tricia. Two Tricias in a small office seemed too much, so she was quickly nicknamed *Little Tricia.*

Little Tricia was young and dating, and often delighted us with short tales of her current beau. Sadly, her mother died from a long battle with breast cancer. To this day I can still remember the day she walked into the office with tears in her eyes and said the ambulance had just left her home as her mom had died. Collectively, the whole office stepped up to embrace her, support her, and help her through this tough time. Like many NCIS offices, we truly operated as a big family.

Two other secretaries in this office were *Evelyn,* a kind woman who bore the same name as my kind mother, and *Deb,* who also volunteered to be a watcher for the birth of a panda at the zoo.

Technology and Investigations

Former NCIS Director SA Tom Betro was interviewed in 2014 and discussed the impact of advancing technologies on the NCIS mission. Excerpts, in his own words, include: Technology has changed the way NCIS and most law enforcement and intelligence organizations do business . . .it is woven into every process and every action that NCIS agents, analysts, and support personnel do every day . . . beginning with evidence collection to computer software and hardware . . . particularly in the areas of forensics, cyber forensics, and digital forensics. . . There is not one single investigation that NCIS works today that does not have a digital component, whether it is a computer, tablet, cell phone, camera, or email. . . Technology has enhanced our ability to accomplish our mission in combat environments . . . due to the threat we are limited by time at crime scenes, but due to technology we can now document and process quickly and get out safely without sacrificing quality. There is room for growth in the area of making retrieval easier in terms of synthesizing and processing quickly the amount of data collected.

Source: [Interview of Betro conducted Feb 19, 2014 by Aaron Sean Poynton for the Domestic Preparedness (DomPrep) Journal]

Mission and Personnel

NCIS has grown from an agency of approximately 500 Special Agents in the 1970s to over 1,000 agents. It currently employs more than 2,000 people, due to the addition of analysts and other technical specialists. NCIS now operates in more than 40 countries and 190 locations.

According to the NCIS current mission statements: "Within the Department of the Navy, the Naval Criminal Investigative Service is the civilian federal law enforcement agency uniquely responsible for investigating felony crime, preventing terrorism and protecting secrets for the Navy and Marine Corps.

NCIS will defeat threats from across the foreign intelligence, terrorist and criminal spectrum by conducting operations and investigations ashore, afloat, and in cyberspace, in order to protect and preserve the superiority of the Navy and Marine Corps warfighters."

+ + + + + +

Cold Case Investigations

Multiple media sources report the NCIS Cold Case Unit (as of 2012) had cracked 63 cases and was working on an additional 40. Media articles frequently mention that NCIS used the Miami-Dade PD protocols established in the 1980s to investigate cold cases, and *became the nation's first agency on the federal level to staff a cold case unit.* Moreover this NCIS Unit has often been asked to conduct training at state, federal, and international levels.

Lawofficer.com reports: "In 1995 . . . NCIS investigated the death of a US Navy crew member in a two-year-old homicide in St. Thomas, US Virgin Islands. A task force of six NCIS Special Agents, five local detectives and a Deputy US Marshal worked around the clock on this unresolved murder and 27 days later, the killer was taken into custody. . . Out of this the cold case unit was born**.**"

In an interview NCIS Unit Supervisor **Mike Keleher** described the three hard protocols for cold case investigation as follows:

1) Relationships change over time i.e. a former friend or relative may now decide to cooperate.

2) New science and forensics are always being developed, i.e. touch DNA from shed skin cells.

3) The solution to a cold case may already be in the file, and all that is needed is a fresh set of eyes.

(Sources:http://www.stripes.com/news/the-real-ncis-years-of-work-dogged-investigations-and-no-promise-of-closure-1.232874 ;http://www.lawofficer.com/ articles/2011/08/ cold-case-homicides.html)

+ + + + + +

A small sampling of these closed investigations include:

-A 40 year old former sailor was arrested in Los Angeles, California 14 years after the murder of **RMSN Pamela Ann Kimbrue** in Norfolk, Virginia. She had been raped, beaten, and murdered. Suspect was convicted in federal court and sentenced to two life terms.

-An active duty Chief Petty Officer was arrested, tried and found guilty 6 years after the murder of **Jean Marie Tehan** in South Carolina. She was beaten and burned beyond recognition and was initially buried as a Jane Doe. Suspect was convicted of murder at a courts martial and sentenced to 30 years.

-In 1998 a USN Petty Officer admitted to the murder 22 years earlier of **Carol Dean Hutto** in Key Largo, Florida; this admission came after the third re-opening of this case. Suspect was extradited to Florida for trial. (Recent media reports he was found guilty of first degree murder, and expected to receive life in prison)

-In May 1997 a suspect was arrested in the death of a dependent wife, **Nancy Fern Pope**, 29 years earlier. She died from stab wounds to her chest; her body was found in her on-base quarters.

-In June 1994 dependent son **Timothy Joseph Ellis, Jr** was transported to the Jacksonville Naval Air Station Emergency Room with head wounds, where he subsequently died. Upon re-opening the case a subject was re-interrogated, admitted culpability, and was given six years confinement by a general courts martial.

-USN officer **Verle Lee Hartley** died in the Naval Regional Medical Center, Jacksonville, Florida in 1982; toxicology reports showed arsenic poisoning. Fourteen years later a suspect (wife) was developed and admitted culpability. (Recent media reports suspect was sentenced to 40 years in prison.)

-An anonymous caller provided a tip to restart the case in the 1994 murder of Robert Stewart, USN. Thirteen years later NCIS agents arrested 35 year old Douglas Hughes and 41 year old Rachelle Reynolds, who each eventually pled guilty to manslaughter, carjacking, kidnapping, and other associated crimes. Hughes was sentenced to 20 years in prison and Reynolds to 11 years.

-The defendant, William Veach, was sentenced in an Arizona court on November 13, 2009 to 10 years in prison following conviction for his part in the death of a 17 month old girl seven years earlier. The infant was the child of defendant's girlfriend at the time, and the defendant was serving in the USMC. The child died from head trauma. Originally claimed as a fall from a high chair, NCIS cold case agents reopened the case and a pediatric ophthalmologist concluded the injuries were from being shaken and not falling from her high chair. Source: *State v. William Veach* www.azag.gov 2010

+ + + + + +

NCIS Contingency Response Field Office (CRFO) Afghanistan 2009

According to **SA Roman Caruso** (in a 2010 article) NCIS has been deploying SAs to Iraq, Afghanistan and the Horn of Africa since 2003. In 2005 NCIS stood up the Contingency Response Field Office (CRFO) whose main mission is to deploy to high-risk environments and accomplish all aspects of the NCIS mission in the same, professional manner as is done elsewhere. The deployments are four to six months. Sa Caruso writes about his most recent deployment as the Supervisory Special Agent (SSA) of the General Crimes unit in Camp Barber and Camp Leatherneck. This comes after previous deployments to both Iraq and Afghanistan.

SA Caruso describes living conditions in Afghanistan as HARD: NCIS has two tents, which SA Caruso states are prone to taking in rain and dust. Office contents consist of wooden planks hammered onto scrap leg supports and one folding Rubbermaid table. Fortunately plenty of bottled water is available because it is necessary to use it for drinking and brushing one's teeth, as accidentally drinking water from the shower leads to bad results! Beds were bunk beds with no mattresses; shower and toilet facilities were a trek through dust and gravel; food was from the military chow hall. A large and very noisy 1970s era diesel-powered generator, on a 440 alternating current, provided power. Everything electronic had to be plugged into a step-down capacitor; unfortunately, says SA Caruso "It took several

SA Roman Caruso, left, with SA Robert Ziegler

spectacular explosions to learn this necessity."

The average workday was 16-17 hours and 90% of it occurred at locations other than Camp Leatherneck. This meant SAs often used helicopters to travel to remote areas. Investigations were sometimes sexual assaults or narcotics, but most efforts were on violations of the laws of armed combat (LOAC). Proficient interview skills were a must, as was the ability to conduct a death crime scene in the allotted

20-30 minutes. On nearly every occasion, coordination occurred via satellite phone and email with **SA Tom Brady**, forensic consultant, of the Southeast Field Office. Agents also had to demonstrate tactical proficiency so the Marines felt comfortable that NCIS SAs would not be a detriment to their mission. In fact, field agents did demonstrate proficiency to the point where the commanders for the Regional Combat Team instructed they be supplied with desert battle dress uniforms and boots. SA Caruso states "I have never experienced the extreme sense of pride as I did watching my fellow NCIS agents being recognized in this manner by the most elite fighting force in the world!"

Late summer sand storm Afghanistan

Special Contingency Group Team One 1995

The Balkans War ended in 1995 after NATO bombed the Bosnian Serbs, and Muslim and Croat Armies made gains on the ground. NCIS sent agents into the area to "provide force protection support to NATO, US Forces, and to augment EUCOM Force Protection Team 40."

The team leader was **SA William "Brook" Heider,,** who led a team of three other agents. Prior to working with NCIS, **SA Heider** was a US Army Ranger. He was hired by NCIS in 1981, and retired in 2013, after serving with NCIS for over 30 years.

SA Heider recalls that he and **SA Rick Parks** deployed for six months to Tuzla, and were attached to the Army MI Battalion for transit into country, commonly called the *Wagon Train from Hell,* with the mud and a hastily constructed pontoon bridge. He notes the *nicer* assignment was in Zagreb, where **SAs Gary VanOrden** and **Valerie Cernosek** were assigned.

Special Agent William "Brook" Heider

Anti-Piracy

In the same interview sourced elsewhere regarding advances in technical applications, **former NCIS Director Tom Betro** discusses the role of NCIS in piracy. Excerpts, in his own words, include: NCIS plays a major role in collecting intelligence . . . investigating acts of piracy . . . and supporting prosecutions of pirates. . . We went to the crime scene of the lifeboat from the *MV Maersk Alabama* (where **Captain Phillips** was held) . . . we did a full crime scene examination and gathered evidence to support prosecution, including forensics, interview, and interrogation. . . NCIS also recently supported the FBI and the Joint Terrorism Task Force in the investigation and prosecution of Somali pirates for acts of piracy against the *USS Ashland (LSD-48)*. This represented the first conviction for piracy in Norfolk, Virginia in more than 150 years. . . SAs work aboard ships tasked with defending the shipping and maritime industry against pirates . . . If you commit an act of piracy NCIS will investigate and support prosecution against you.

A more expansive article was written by **Deedra Allison**, assigned to the Multiple Threat Alert Center (MTAC) at NCISHQ. She interview several NCIS agents and delineates NCIS anti-piracy efforts in the article.

SA Matt Butler, of the Middle East Field Office in Bahrain, has been part of the counter-piracy efforts since 2006, and he says *"We're it – the only law enforcement agency embarked on Navy ships to deal with this."* To understand the scope of these efforts one can learn much from reading about the NCIS involvement in the widely publicized piracy of the *Maersk Alabama* and hostage Captain Richard

Phillips. What follows is a short list of this involvement as noted by author Allison:

-April 8, 2009: 4 Somali pirates boarded the *Maersk Alabama,* a US flagged container ship with a crew of 20 American merchant marines. Captain Richard Phillips was taken hostage and all four pirates eventually escaped aboard the ship's encapsulated lifeboat.

-*USS Bainbridge (DDG-96)* located 300 nautical miles away was dispatched to the scene along with the *USS Halyburton (FFG-40)* and *USS Boxer (LHD-4).* **SA John Swanson,** based in the Singapore Field Office, was aboard the *USS Boxer, (LHD-4),* as was **Special Agent Afloat Noel Zuniga.**

-Personnel aboard the *USS Bainbridge* were communicating with the pirates and **SA Joel Mullen**, an experienced hostage negotiator, briefed naval leaders and personnel aboard this warship. These negotiations played out for several days until negotiations broke down. At this time one pirate – who had been stabbed in the hand initially - was aboard the *USS Bainbridge* seeking medical care and assist with negotiations.

-April 12, 2009: SEAL snipers shot and killed three pirates in the encapsulated lifeboat saving the life of Captain Phillips.

-**SA Swanson** interviewed CAPT Phillips immediately following his rescue, and the next day took an inflatable boat out to the lifeboat where the hostage scene played out. He conducted a thorough crime scene examination.

-**SA Zuniga** assisted in the transfer of the surviving pirate to the FBI for ultimate prosecution in New York. On May 18, 2010, he pled guilty and received a 33 year sentence for piracy, kidnapping, and related charges.

--**SAs Ed Jones and Keith Allen** were on temporary duty in Nairobi, Kenya. They boarded the *Maersk Alabama* in Mombasa, Kenya, to debrief the crew. They were assisted by agents from Djibouti. Critical intelligence and information was obtained, passed on to naval leaders, and ultimately incorporated into rescue plans.

Of additional interest in this article is discussion about the huge task of protecting the vast ocean from pirates. The Combined Maritime Forces (CMF) consisting of more than 20 nations created Combined Task Force (CTF) 151 tasked with deterring, disrupting, and suppressing piracy around the Horn of Africa. The first NCIS SA assigned to CTF 151 was **SA Keith Allen.**

+ + + + + +

Depth & Breadth of NCIS Employee service

[Author's note: NCIS employees often come from families with generational military or law enforcement service. They also often serve their communities in many ways during and after retirement. Years ago some chose to contribute to an historical attempt to collect this information. Of those who contributed, what follows is a sampling. It is interesting to know the depths of NCIS employee patriotism and community service, both in work and in volunteerism. The following will give the reader great insight.]

SA Dan Foley: I joined the Navy as a Seaman Recruit in June 1956 and retired as a Colonel, USMCR in June 1998 . Other than a 7 year hiatus after being hired as a civilian SA with ONI in June 1963, I always carried a military ID, including 12 years of active duty. During WWII my father, his brother, and six of my mother's brothers all served. They served in the Army, Navy, and Marine Corps in Great Britain, Europe, North Africa, and the Pacific.

SA Bob Powers: I was a product of ROTC; after college I spent two years on active duty as a US Army LT in Germany before joining

NCIS as an agent. My older brother was a career Army Intelligence Officer, and he was assigned in Saigon when I reported to the NCIS office in Danang. Several months later my younger brother, who was a Marine LCPL, was assigned to an AMTRAK unit in I Corps. I managed to visit with both of them during my tour, but they were unable to make personal contact while they were both in Vietnam. I never thought too much about the three of us being in Vietnam at the same time, until I had a son of my own, and realized how my mother and father must have felt.

SA Jerry Nance: I left a job teaching High School to join the Marines as an Infantry Officer from 1969-1974. In 1974, at the rank of Captain, I left the Marines to join NCIS. Since retiring in 1998, I have been a consultant / case manager for the *National Center for Missing and Exploited Children* for cold cases and child homicide. Six of my cousins all ended up as Firemen; one of the six a paramedic. Four of the six, plus one who was not a fireman, served in the military. I was the only Marine; two were in the Navy and three in the Army.

SA Todd Hannah: I was serving in the Marine Corps at Camp Lejeune, NC when I initiated my application for ONI. I started with ONI in Jan 1957. I remained in the US Marine Corps Reserves. I served a total of 29 years in the reserves and 26 years in law enforcement.

My son, Craig Hannah, was employed as a fingerprint technician by the FBI, then became a police officer with the DC Metropolitan Transit Authority, and ultimately retired as a US Customs Agent. He has three sons (my grandsons), Daniel, Mark and David, all of whom are now serving in the Marine Corps. My granddaughter is marred to an El Paso, TX police officer. My daughter is married to an Ocala, FL Police officer who previously served in the U.S. Air Force.

SA Bill Holt: I received an officer-agent direct commission as an Ensign in 1988 (due to a federal law enforcement background) under a Cold War Navy program that involved only an abbreviated Officer Candidate School of two weeks .I currently work as a Police Senior Training Technician in the Office of Public Safety, New York State Division of Criminal Justice Services.

My brother, Andrew, was commissioned through NROTC and spent 10 years on active duty as a naval aviator flying the P-3. My father, Willard, enlisted in the Navy in 1943 at age 17, and was accepted into the new construction battalions as a "Seabee" Fireman Apprentice . After his service tours, he attended the University of New Hampshire under the GI Bill and graduated as a mechanical engineer. He spent his career designing nuclear reactors for Navy submarines.

My grandfather, also Willard, enlisted as a private in the regular 49th Infantry in 1917 and served in France as part of the American Expeditionary Force (AEF) .

SA Allen Carballo: I served as a SA from 1975 through retirement in 2004. My father-in-law is **SA John (Jack) W . Lynch** who served with NIS/ONI from Nov 1954 to retirement in Nov 1976. Jack Lynch was also a Naval Officer who served from 1933 to 1954 . He was aboard several ships during WWII and served aboard an aircraft carrier during the Korean war .

SA Mike Hawkins: I was a Reserve Officer/Agent operating out of NCIS Charleston . At the same time I was a GM-1811-14 Senior Criminal Investigator at FLETC in Glynco , Georgia, where I taught in both the Legal and Behavioral Science Divisions . While there I was assigned as an Instructor at the International Law Enforcement Academy in Budapest, Hungary, where I trained officers from the former Soviet Bloc countries .

Prior to my Federal service I was a South Carolina State Constable. My wife was a Special Agent with the VA-OIG and my sister-in-law is a detective with the Bellingham, Washington Police Department. My nephew is a uniform patrol officer with the Paterson, New Jersey Police Department.

SA Dennis Usrey: I worked on the Newport, California Police Department before transferring to ONI as an agent in San Francisco, California. I retired from NCIS 28 years later. I subsequently worked with the San Diego Narcotic Information Network, with the California Bureau of Narcotic Enforcement, and as Program Manager for the LInX system in California.

SA Kim (Myers) Usrey: Wife of **SA Dennis Usrey**, worked in the San Diego, California and Norfolk, Virginia areas with NCIS. Her father, Norman Myers, was an aircraft mechanic with the US Air Force in the early 1950s. The Usrey's children include a son who is a San Diego, California Police Officer and reservist in the US Coast Guard, and a daughter who is an FBI Intelligence Analyst married to a DEA Agent.

SA Charlie Roberts: My father joined the Navy in Aug 1941, and was assigned aboard the *USS Yorktown* (CV-5) as a Gunner's Mate Striker . During the spring and summer of 1942, the USS Yorktown was damaged during the Battle of Coral Sea and sunk during the Battle of Midway . Dad then served aboard the *USS Oglala* (LST-1) until the end of the War. Subsequently Dad was a county Sheriff. I have five brothers, four of whom served in the US Navy, and three of whom also served and retired from federal or local law enforcement.

SA Tricia Mansell (author): My father was a Supply Sergeant who served in the Army in both the European Theater and the Pacific Theater in WWII. My father-in-law was a Marine who fought in the Pacific in WWII, and was wounded at the Battle of Saipan. My

73

husband is a US Naval Academy graduate and a now-retired Navy Commander. Prior to NCIS I served as an active duty naval intelligence officer, and continued serving in that capacity as a naval reservist.

SA Ken Lord: I am a retired Lieutenant Colonel, Military Police Corps, US Army reserve. My father, Colonel Kenneth P Lord, Jr .served in the European Theater in WWII. My grandfather, Brigadier General Kenneth P Lord, served in WWI and WWII . My great-grandfather Brigadier General Herbert M . Lord, served pre-WWI and during WWI .

SA John Patrick (Jack) O'Connor: I served both as a NCIS SA and also a Marine Corps officer. My father served in the navy beginning in 1944, and then followed that with 33 years serving with the New Jersey State Police. My grandfather served in the navy in WWI and then rejoined to serve again during WWII.

SA John "Jack" O'CONNOR: I served as an NCIS Special Agent from 1984-2010, and before that I was a US Marine Corps officer. My father served in the US Navy during WWII, and then worked for 33 years with the New Jersey State Police. My grandfather served in the Navy in both WWI and WWII. My brother retired as a LTCOL from the US Marine Corps.

SA John Harris: Volunteers for *Team Adam, National Center for Missing and Exploited Children.*

SA Kenneth Lord: Volunteers for the organization Vets with a Mission.

SA Herman Hughes: Serves as Chaplain for the Lake County, California *United Veterans council Funeral Honors Team.*

SA David Watson: Serves on the Board of Directors of the *Herbert Ford Memorial Museum in Homer, Louisiana*. Also assists with f*und raising for a local hospital* and with the *Men's Christian Action Team* to build handicap ramps for elderly citizens.

SA Tom Kellerhals: Works for local *Volunteer Fire Department.*

SA Rick Machin: Volunteers at an *elementary school* in his hometown and also is on the Board of the *San Juan Preservation Trust*, which is a land conservation organization.

SA George Reis: Serves as a docent for the *San Diego Museum of Art*, volunteers as a Ranger for the *US National Park Service.*

SA Gordon Crossman: Volunteers to serve meals for both *Meals-on-Wheels* and the *Salvation Army.*

SA Leo Barron: Volunteers to plan Mass and Ecumenical Service for the *Law Enforcement Community in Connecticut* and surrounding areas. Delivers food to a mission and volunteers to assist in the *Special Olympics.*

SA Ed Coyle: Voluneers as a *Boy Scout Leader.*

SA Alan Sipe: Volunteers as a *Retired Senior Volunteer Patrol Officer* with the San Diego, California Police Department.

SA Joe Beene: Volunteers as an usher at the *Barn's of Wolf Trap and Ford's Theater*. Sings in a choir and plays musical instruments for schools and nursing homes. Acts as a *Scoutmaster* specializing in leading high adventure backpacking and canoeing trips.

SA Darryl Toler: Is President of the local *hospital auxiliary* and *teaches Sunday school*.

SA Larry Ferrell: Volunteers *transporting patients to hospital*

SA Robin Parks: Volunteers at *animal shelters for lions and other big cats,* which has led to his service with law enforcement agencies and the *Mountain Lion Foundation*. He consults on strategy to deal with the balance of preservation and safety for big cats and humans.

Chapter 5: **Criminal Cases**

The below case summaries and memories are offered, in no particular order, as a sampling of crimes investigated by NCIS through the years.

SA Blair Gluba writes that this investigation "begins with the Prince William County PD (PWPD), Virginia and ends in Tokyo, Japan. Family members who were unable to contact Ms. Su Chou Thomas were worried and contacted PWPD. On January 31,1982 a search of her residence in Virginia turned up her dead body and missing expensive jewelry. Ms. Thomas was a Japanese citizen who visited Japan several times a year on business. Found at the crime scene was a business card with the inscription "Pearl Shop, Ginza, Tokyo Japan" and printed in pencil was *"Miss Sugar"*. In Japanese, sugar translates to the name SATO, a common Japanese family name.

A search of local pawn shops discovered a Rolex belonging to the victim and pawned by USMC Sergeant Timothy Dale Bunch. Sgt Bunch had a history: He was caught in an NCIS drug suppression op, subsequently agreed to work as a confidential informant, transferred to Japan for his personal protection after several arrests were made with his assistance, and during the time of the murder he was back in Quantico, Virginia as a prosecution witness. While there, he mailed a package to his mother living in Kentucky; when recovered by PWPD this package was found to contain the murder weapon and stolen jewelry.

NCIS Yokosuka office agents **Blair Gluba** and **Koje Watanabe** were tasked to find *"Miss Sugar"*. They requested local assistance and 200 local detectives flooded the Ginza district with them in search of *Miss Sugar*. In short order she was found and interviewed at Tokyo PD headquarters. She recalled the victim and remembered selling her jewelry, including a pearl ring with a custom mounting.

By this time suspect Sgt Bunch was back in Japan. PWPD sent a detective and an attorney from Virginia to Japan to interrogate and arrest Sgt Bunch. A command authorized search of his quarters turned up $20,000 worth of jewelry stolen from the victim, including the pearl ring. Sgt Bunch was arrested and escorted back to Virginia for trial. He was sentenced to death for the murder of Ms. Su Chou Thomas, and following a number of appeals, executed in 1991."

+ + + + + +

NCIS Operations Scoutmaster and Stableboy

SA George McClellan was assigned with NCIS in Subic Bay, Republic of the Philippines in the early 1970s. He writes: *"Operation Scoutmaster* was introduced in the Philippines in 1971 as a proactive measure to fight the volumes of materials being stolen from the Subic Bay base. SAs were located in a classified space in the building housing NCIS Subic Bay. SAs were recruited to mix and mingle in an undercover capacity with the locals, choosing their own hours of work, developing their own methodologies for collecting information, recruiting their own sources. Each major command on base was assigned one Scoutmaster Agent. The pattern of theft quickly became clear. Gangs of organized crime were embedded as employees on the base, and used secret compartments to carry away stolen property, especially from the Naval Exchange warehouses. The Ship Repair Facility and dock yards were mostly attacked at night by the sea, with thieves using banca boats (silent dugout canoes)."

SA George McClellan advises that "about a year and a half into the Scoutmaster operation, realizing the tremendous success, proactive techniques were designed to target foreign port visits as they pertain to narcotics trafficking to sailors. This became *Operation Stableboy*. The techniques were simple: Knowing port visit schedules in advance, a n NCIS agent would visit the area when a US navy ship was conducting a port visit. The agent would work with local police to arrest narcotics sellers by using NCIS undercover buyers and NCIS money to make buys, and then immediately signal local officials to make an arrest of the seller. Thus, narcotic sales were controlled to lessen the chance of sales to sailors on shore leave. These proactive techniques were applied to port visits in Hong Kong; Bangkok and Pattaya Beach, Thailand; Karachi, Pakistan; and Cebu, Republic of the Philippines."

SA **John Morgan** writes that : he and **SA John Cusack** were the first agents assigned to *Operation Stableboy*. The first drug buy originated from drug intelligence gathered by a great informant from Operation Scoutmaster. It occurred in Olongapo, outside of Subic Bay Naval Station, circa 1972. Others assisting were **SAs Bob Brady**, **Don Webb**, and **Michael B. Jones**, - all of Scoutmaster fame. This buy was of a large brick of morphine the dealer was selling for $1K. After the drug and money swap the dealer was arrested, but not before he gave quite a struggle including attempting to get a large knife out of his pocket."

+ + + + + +

In an article written by NCIS **SA Byron Taylor,** he notes: *The basic operations used in Scoutmaster and Stableboy were followed early on in developing proactive fraud investigations.* The fraud program was born out of the 1970's attention given to *fraud, waste, and abuse* within the federal government. Initial fraud efforts by NCIS had limited success; they included training at supply centers and awareness programs. What remained of these programs were twenty five SAs scattered throughout NCIS with fraud training. What evolved was a manual authored by **SA Bobby Brady** (to include proactive efforts made successful in *Scoutmaster* and *Stableboy*), plus extensive support from then NCIS management: **SA J. Brian McKee** and **RADM Irish Flynn**. This led to dedicated careers and commitment in combatting fraud. And it led to success.

NCIS **SA Byron Taylor** writes of an operation initiated by NCIS in the fall of 1986, and then joined by the FBI. Widespread fraud was uncovered regarding illegally providing competitor's bids for DoD contracts. The investigation disclosed that Mr. William Parkin, who had retired as the Executive Director of the Acquisition for the Joint Cruise Missile Project Office in November 1983, became a consultant. As a consultant he served as a middleman who paid government employees for procurement of sensitive information, and then sold this information to contractors. The investigation included electronic intercepts authorized initially by the US District Court for the Eastern District of Virginia, and with evidence developed from these intercepts, widespread intercepts were authorized.

At the peak of this operation 26 NCIS agents and 65 FBI agents were dedicated full time. On June 14, 1988, NCIS and the FBI executed 46 search warrants in 12 states simultaneously. The Department of Justice (DOJ) dedicated ten attorneys to prosecute these cases. DoD provided three military JAG attorneys, eleven Navy contract specialists, three auditors, four contract lawyers, and three administrative support personnel.

As a result, fifty-three individuals and nine corporations were convicted of various crimes ranging from bribery to tax evasion. They were sentenced to a total of 809 months confinement and seventy-nine years of probation. The total criminal penalties were over $250 million. This was one of the biggest fraud cases in history.

+ + + + + +

On December 20, 1977, a Philippine National entered the Prudential Bank aboard the US Naval Base at Subic Bay, Republic of the Philippines. This man displayed a shotgun, announced a robbery, and said he had a bomb. He refused to allow anyone to leave the bank; his hostages were all Philippine nationals. His demand was for a helicopter. NCIS hostage negotiations began quickly and lasted 44 hours. The situation was resolved when some hostages attacked the captor killing him. One shot was fired by the hostages and then all inside fled.

+ + + + + +

The following case summary is extracted from an article written by **SA Claude Rollins** about an NCIS task force assembled in 1991 when he was the NCIS Regional Director in Norfolk, Virginia:

When the carrier *USS Enterprise (CVN-65)* was in Newport News , Virginia dry dock for the most extensive and expensive refit ever attempted (cost $1.5 billion) a couple of small trash fires were set.

Investigation initially showed there had been as many as 25 such fires in recent years not reported to NCIS, after which the ship advised they could not proceed with fueling the ship's eight reactors unless and until the arsonist was caught and the fires stopped.

The NCIS task force was headed by **SA James Coady,** from the NCIS Oceana, Virginia office. Other members from the Tidewater area were **SAs Tony Suchy**, **Bill Heath**, and **Scott James**. They began with about 5,000 potential suspects but were able to narrow that down to 900 based on FBI profiling. The agents worked with the ship to develop a system to scan and trace entry and exit of all personnel. Looking backwards in time, they combed personnel records and the scenes of previous arsons aboard this ship. They received a great break when interviewing a crew member who recalled seeing a sailor fleeing the scene of an area subsequently discovered to have a burning trash fire. The sailor could not identify the fleeing suspect, but through hypnosis was able to provide a detailed description as well as four letters of the name stenciled above the sailor's shirt pocket. That information plus a lineup led to positive identification of the arsonist.

During interrogation the suspect denied involvement and sought an attorney. Continuing investigation was sufficient to close the case as it revealed the suspect's work and watch schedule matched the trash can fires, aspects of his clothing matched material found at a fire scene, and his former employer in Florida was interviewed and advised the suspect had set small trash fires in the supermarket where he worked.

The *Enterprise* Commanding Officer later invited the Task Force agents and other NCIS interested parties to a meeting where he gave their wives flowers and the SAs letters of commendation. During his remarks he discussed the many people who had served the *Enterprise* during this historic yard period, but his greatest gratitude went to the NCIS Task Force. As Claude Rollins recalls, the CO said the NCIS

Task Force " . . . gave him the greatest service; the return of safety to his crew."

In March 1989 USMC Captain Shirley Russell disappeared. **NCIS SA Joanne M. Jensen** led a two year joint NCIS / FBI investigative team in what became a homicide investigation. Captain Russell's body was never found, though her husband Robert P. Russell was convicted of her murder in Federal court on May 3, 1991. It was the first Federal homicide case successfully prosecuted without a body in modern history (some states' courts had tried murder cases without a body).

On March 12, 1990 USMC Lance Corporal Jeffrey A. Borchers was killed as he stood watch at the main entry gate of the Commander-in-Chief, US Pacific Fleet in Pearl Harbor, Hawaii. His service pistol was stolen from him and used to murder him. **NCIS SA Steven Matteson** solved this case through careful investigation and a search warrant which led to discovery of spent shell casings in suspect's back yard. These casings were a match to the Corporal's pistol. A plaque was later placed on this gate to honor victim: According to a news article in the local newspaper, the convicted killer, Wendell Pichay, is serving a life sentence without parole.

SA Tricia Mansell (author): I got a call after midnight from the duty SA, who asked me to go to the Balboa Naval Hospital in San Diego, California and interview victims in the emergency room. There had been a riot on the Coronado base which started in the enlisted club and spilled over the entire base. There were three distinct groups in the club that evening: enlisted sailors who were assigned to a submarine tender at Pt. Loma; enlisted sailors assigned to Coronado; and enlisted Army reservists from a unit in El Centro, California who were in the area for drills. The riot took on the tone of Army vs. Navy, but also a racial tone of White vs. Hispanic. The racial overtone was because most of the sailors were White and the Army Reservists were Hispanic.

The duty agent asked me to go to Balboa Hospital ER to interview eight men who had been taken there with stab wounds. This wasn't an easy task for me and I learned some new things about investigative work that night. In the ER the doctors and nurses are completely devoted to saving lives, as they should be. These eight victims were in various conditions, with some being moderately injured and others critically injured. Most stabbings seemed to be in the torso; many victims had innards hanging out. Some were awake and coherent and others were not.

I attempted to interview the victims who were coherent, but in doing so I had to get to the victim who was inside a circle of doctors and nurses surrounding the patient. I felt intrusive, and my work felt minimally important compared to their lifesaving work. I quickly determined multiple men were stabbed in a riot in the dark of night where one or more people brought a knife to a fistfight. No one I was able to speak with knew or could even describe exactly who stabbed them in the riotous atmosphere of darkness.

The victims were Army Reservists, meaning the knife attacks came from one or more sailors. Identifying the specific suspects who used knives did come later, through individual interviews of the many sailors present.

+ + + + + +

February 1986: A Petty Officer was sentenced to death at a General Court Martial following successful prosecution for his stabbing to death his Division Officer while their ship was underway from Bermuda to Nova Scotia. NCIS SAs recognized include **SAs Kent Walker, Dale Laing, Doug Gallant, Beverly Hack, Paul Jordan, Leon Dresek, Mark Clookie, Mike Lawrence and Reserve SA Pete Pascuicco**.

October 21, 1979: NCIS office Jacksonville was completely gutted by fire. **SA Dan McBride** wrote an article describing NCIS SAs being awakened early that Sunday morning to respond to a suspected arson of their office spaces. In fact, everything burned: walls, equipment, all files except those in fireproof cabinets – everything! In short order two military and one civilian suspect emerged. These were three interrelated lesbian females who were targeting NCIS due to their frustration of facing imminent discharge after admitting lesbian activity to SAs. Until new facilities could be acquired, SAs conducted interviews in, as **SA McBride** puts it "in the new ventilated NCIS Jacksonville interrogation space, under a pine tree, in an open area adjacent to the remains of the burned building". All three suspects eventually pled guilty, although there was considerable finger pointing, confessions and recanting, evidence of drug and alcohol involvement, and fighting amongst themselves. All three had a black eye caused by the others during the act of committing arson. All three suspects were successfully prosecuted in Federal court.

+ + + + + +

SA Blair Gluba wrote an article about the use of hypnosis in investigations, a technique usually reserved for use when all others fail, and administered by a mental health professional. SA Gluba describes in detail one NCIS murder investigation that was solved when the time frame was narrowed due to witness memories under hypnosis.

+ + + + + +

On June 13, 2015, multinational Combined Task Force 150 (CTF-150), with assistance from a NCIS Middle East Field Office Special Agent, intercepted a fishing vessel off the coast of Somalia and seized 118 kilograms of heroin, which has a US street value of $48,144,000. At the time of the seizure the Special Agent was serving patrol assignment aboard the Royal New Zealand Navy warship *Te Kaha* as part of *Operation Dirty Dhow*, providing law enforcement expertise to the commanding officer of the frigate. The agent supervised the flag verification boarding of vessel, which was determined to be stateless. A search of the vessel revealed the heroin concealed in hidden compartments. . . Earlier that same month two NCIS Special Agents assisted in three seizures that yielded 401 kilograms of heroin, which has a US street value of $163,608,000.

On April 15, 2015, Garrett Wiseman was sentenced to five years in prison and three years of supervised release. He pled guilty in US District Court for his role in an assault in connection to an employee kickback scheme being investigated by NCIS. In 2010, NCIS and the Department of Labor Inspector General initiated a joint investigation into Sands Mechanical Inc., a subcontractor on the multi-million dollar restoration and rehabilitation of the Marine Corps Reserve Training

Center at Joint Base-McGuire-Dix-Lakehurst in Burlington County, N.J.

On April 17, 2015, retired US Air Force Senior Master Sergeant Christopher Underwood was sentenced to 24 months and 1 day in prison and 3 years of supervised release after pleading guilty to 1 count of wire fraud and 24 counts of aggravated identity theft. An NCIS investigation revealed Underwood stole personal and government travel cards and personal effects from unsecured backpacks, vehicles, and lockers at base gyms aboard Naval Medical Center San Diego, Marine Corps Recruit Depot San Diego, Marine Corps Air Station Miramar, and Marine Corps Base Camp Pendleton.

In 1997 a case was opened by **SA Paul Graf** of the NCIS office in Northeastern US. SA Graf was later assisted by **SA David Watson** of the NCIS Singapore office, as well as elements of the DEA in Bangkok, Thailand. The case was later named *Operation Deep Sea*. SA Graf opened an online operation designed to identify and prosecute Naval affiliated child molesters and a suspect was developed. Suspect was assigned to communications aboard a US Navy Attack Submarine in the Pacific. After some communication, suspect stopped corresponding and the case was closed. Nine months later suspect again contacted SA Graf requesting assistance arranging sexual molestation of an eleven year old Thai girl while he vacationed in Pattaya Beach, Thailand. Suspect wanted to produce child pornography for resale in the US

Suspect requested information about getting a date rape drug in Pattaya Beach, along with Valium and Ether, without a prescription. **SA Watson** conducted liaison with the US Embassy, Thailand and

DEA, and a meet was arranged. Suspect showed up, once again explained his intentions to undercover role players, and was arrested.

Of interest is that suspect was an exceptional software designer, and had obtained USN permission to install his email-enabling software aboard his assigned Submarine. As a result, many of the final emails between SA Graf and suspect were actually transmitted to and received from suspect while he was aboard the submarine operating deep below the Pacific Ocean.

Suspect was interrogated by **SA Watson** and made a videotaped confession. He was prosecuted by a General Court-Martial in Hawaii. He was convicted and sentenced to three years in prison and made to register as a sex offender. **Suspect was the first US citizen ever prosecuted under assimilated Federal Law prohibiting overseas travel ("…in foreign commerce") with the intent to sexually molest a child.** NCIS **SA's Graf and Watson**, along with elements of DEA and the Royal Thai Police Officers, were subsequently nominated for the Federal Law Enforcement Officer Association (FLEOA) International Teamwork Award.

+ + + + + +

SA Tom Cavanagh submitted information about a case he was involved with when he was at NCIS New York (1982-1984). The supervisor was **SA Al Maretta.** SA Cavanagh was assigned to investigate fraud at the Naval Resale Supply Office (NAVRESO) located then at Fort Wadsworth on Staten Island, New York. He learned of several cost overruns in the project brought to the attention of Rear Admiral Wilson, then CO of NAVRESSO. Initial inquiries identified the budget for renovation originally set at 3 million dollars had ballooned to almost 8 million dollars. Subsequent investigation grew from a one agent case to a task force, and became what was then the largest white collar fraud case in the history of NCIS.

The investigation included the first ever Federal Grand Jury for NCIS, the first ever use of **Racketeer Influenced and Corrupt Organization** Act (RICO) in NCIS (with the Department of the Navy as the criminal enterprise used) and concluded with a conviction of Louis J Blanco, the NAVRESSO Project manager. His $750K house in NJ was seized, along with its contents (to include countless works of art and even a "steam mood enclosure shower room with Bose stereo and a recliner").

The case gathered national headlines at the time and ended up with contracting firms in every discipline (electric, plumbing, masonry, painting, carpentry) getting convicted of paying kickbacks to Mr. Blanco totaling in the millions of dollars. Mr. Blanco was convicted of RICO and the contractors all were convicted of felony bribery charges. It was called by the then US Attorney Andrew Maloney the worst case of such fraud he had ever seen.

+ + + + + +

SA Cavanagh advises that another significant NCIS case involved the conviction of Brooklyn Congressman Fred Richmond on federal corruption charges that included payment of an illegal gratuity to a Brooklyn Naval Yard employee. He funneled payment to the employee using a fake college scholarship fund.

Chapter 6: **Foreign Counterintelligence (FCI)**

Espionage effects every American. Not only are US military men and women put at risk, but America's strategic plans are exposed and our armament technologies are compromised. Americans pay millions of dollars through taxes to develop platforms and missiles to ensure our own military might; espionage comes down to theft. In many cases this theft requires our taxpayers to pay more money for engineering new replacements and / or developing new strategies.

President Franklin D. Roosevelt signed a memorandum on 26 June, 1939 stating it was his desire that *"investigation of all espionage, counter-espionage, and sabotage be controlled and handled by the Federal Bureau of Investigation...the Military Intelligence Division of the War Department ....and the Office of Naval Intelligence (ONI) of the Navy Department."* The ONI counter-intelligence mission led to a post WWII expansion of this ONI unit to include felony case investigations. Following that, in 1966, this ONI unit broke away to form NIS, leading to NCIS.

While spying has been around forever, in modern times the 1980s have been historically notated as the *Decade of Spy*. More specifically, 1985 has been called the *Year of the Spy,* in part because of the huge impact of the John *Walker Spy Ring* and the *Jonathan Pollard* case.

The US Navy was the most heavily targeted of military services, probably because our Navy possesses tremendous mobile, maritime power. This sea power extends to land with aircraft carrier strike forces and missiles launched from surface warships and silent submarines. Naval Special Forces are considered by some to be the best in the world. All-in-all it makes sense any enemy would consider classified material held by our naval personnel valuable.

Espionage investigations and double agent (DA) operations have several objectives, chief among them is to stop the leaking of classified material to a foreign country. Another objective is determining the type and extent of damage to naval systems and strategy caused by espionage. This is known as *damage assessment* and it plays a huge role in the investigative process.

What follows in some depth are samples of those investigations and operations that made national news, set legal precedents, or are uniquely interesting.

ESPIONAGE INVESTIGATIONS

Nelson Cornelius Drummond: This USN sailor was recruited by the Soviets while stationed in London in 1958 to provide them with classified information. An FBI / ONI investigation resulted in his arrest in September of 1962 in a New York diner. Drummond was in the company of two known Soviet military intelligence officers; classified material was recovered. He was found guilty in Federal Court and sentenced to life in prison. A *damage assessment estimated it would cost the US $200 million dollars* to recover from damage done by Drummond's espionage activities.

\+ \+ \+ \+ \+ \+

Brian Patrick Horton: The *Horton Clause* is a legal technique named after him. It allows for damage assessment to be considered after the prosecution phase. In return, this entices the suspect to cooperate under a post-trial grant of immunity in an effort to reduce his sentence. In 1982 Horton was a navy intelligence specialist assigned to a Fleet Intelligence Center in Norfolk, Virginia. He was convicted at a General Court Martial on counts of failure to report contacts with hostile country nationals and solicitation to commit espionage. He was sentenced to six years confinement at hard labor.

\+ \+ \+ \+ \+ \+

John Anthony Walker, Jr.: A USN Chief Warrant Officer, he was arrested on May 20, 1985, during the course of his espionage activities in Maryland. *A joint NCIS / FBI investigation revealed he was the center of a spy ring.* He began his espionage activities in 1968, and along the way he recruited his brother Arthur Walker (USN Commander), his son Michael (USN sailor), his friend Jerry Whitworth (USN Senior Chief) and he attempted to recruit a daughter serving in the US Army. Both John Walker and Jerry Whitworth served in the field of communications with high level access to a broad range of material; their damage, in particular, was considerable. John Walker compromised encryption keys which directly led to compromise of a million classified messages, and that was just a part of the loss to the US military through his years of his spying. All men in this spy ring were convicted of espionage related charges. John was sentenced to two life terms plus ten years; he served his time at the Federal Correctional Complex in Butner NC and died there in August 2014. Brother Arthur died at the same prison complex one month earlier, in July 2014. Son Michael served fifteen years in prison and was released in 2000. Jerry Whitworth was sentenced to 365 years in prison. As of this publication date he is now over 80 years old and still serving his time at the Federal Penitentiary in Atwater, CA.

[Author's note: At the time this investigation was the largest to date in the history of NCIS due to the number of suspects over decades of spying, and it was the first investigation to be computerized for case control. Driving this case was the navy's attempt to get an accurate damage assessment. A task force was assembled in the office of then Director of Naval Intelligence (DNI), Admiral William Studeman. Virtually all NCIS offices ended up working leads; some offices worked a considerable amount. **SA Alan Sipe** *was the case supervisor at NCIS HQ, and worked for* **SA Jim Austin**. *The NCIS office in Norfolk, Virginia had field control under* **SA Tom Boley.** *Eventually the San Francisco NCIS office became heavily involved, and SAs* **Bill Wittenberger** *and* **Wanda Simmon** *were involved. Also heavily involved were* **SA George Bedway** *at NCIS HQ and* **SA Keith Hitt,** *who interrogated subject Michael Walker aboard a deployed aircraft carrier.* **Tricia Mansell** *(author) worked multiple duties at NCIS Headquarters, to include: designing the computer tracking, helping to supervise the investigative leads needed, working closely with the damage assessment task force, and playing a key role in the subsequent Stillwell Commission convened to study espionage.]*

Many NCIS SAs could write a book just about their own involvement in this investigation. **SA Brian Cashman** worked on this case under **SA Tom Boley** out of NCIS Norfolk where a large NCIS / FBI task force was formed to search John Walker's home, plane, houseboat, and business office. SA **Cashman's** memory of the home search is insightful; excerpts are included here: ***"At approximately 3:00PM our team arrived at Walker's home. There was a tremendous network media response to Walker's arrest and media*** *trucks choked the streets near his house. We had so many agents at the back door waiting to sign-in, as each agent did, the deck collapsed under the load. In a remarkably short time, I mean minutes, a carpenter was recruited to re-attach the deck. The carpenter seemed to come from nowhere... Groups of four mixed FBI / NCIS agents searched each room. Each room was cut into quadrants. Each agent searched his square or quadrant until each agent was satisfied their quarter was completely searched. Then we shifted quadrants in the room and searched again. We did that four times until each section had been searched four times. . . . It took time. Agent teams then switched rooms and we searched the quadrants again! Four more times. We switched rooms all night. . . . Among items discovered by all, I am proud to say that after others had searched one area, when it was my turn, I found shoeboxes full of receipts indicating travel related to espionage activities. John Walker had purchased gas in places like Montreal, Mexico, and Austria. In fact, these receipts were a "Trip-Ticket" that would be of great assistance in solving this investigation."*

Jonathan Jay Pollard: He worked as *a civilian intelligence analyst for the Naval Intelligence Command (NIC) beginning in 1980. In 1984 he transferred to NCIS Headquarters* where he worked as an analyst in the Anti-Terrorism Alert Center (ATAC). On November 21, 1985 he was arrested for espionage after his coworkers' suspicions led to an NCIS investigation. From 1984 until the time of his arrest in 1985 he passed classified information to his handler in Israeli intelligence. He plead guilty to espionage and was sentenced to life imprisonment. He was incarcerated at the Butler Federal Correction

Complex in North Carolina. After 30 years in prison, he was released in November 2015, but required to have 5 more years on parole. When that time expired in 2020, Pollard and his second wife moved to Israel.

His wife at the time of his arrest (Ann Henderson Pollard) also plead guilty and was sentenced to five years in prison. She was released after two years and eight months from the Federal Prison at Danbury, Connecticut. She has been living in Israel since 2010. Jonathan and Anne Pollard divorced and Jonathan remarried. While in prison. **SA Ron Olive**, the Wash D. C. NCIS field office case supervisor, has written a book that details his recollections of this investigation.

When Pollard was arrested for espionage he was an NCIS employed analyst. The fact that Pollard's spying was for Israel did not mitigate his illegal activity. Though he initially claimed he spied for ideological reasons, the investigation showed his actions quickly turned into *information provided for money,* a common 1980s era motive.

Of note is the ***Stilwell Commission*** (General Richard G. Stilwell, US Army, Chairman) was convened in Washington D. C. to study the espionage problem, delineate findings and implement recommendations to better guard our nation's secrets. NCIS **SA Lanny McCullough** chaired the umbrella committee within NCIS. Recommendations by this Commission included tightening access controls, strengthening background investigations, expanding polygraph examinations, etc.

+ + + + + +

Sergeant Clayton John Lonetree: While serving as a USMC Embassy Guard in Moscow (beginning in 1984) he had an affair with a Russian woman who led him to a Soviet Intelligence agent. He *compromised data on American intelligence agents and information on the US Embassies in Moscow and Vienna.* In 1987 he was convicted of espionage and sentenced to 30 years in prison. *He was the first United States Marine ever convicted of espionage.*

This investigation followed right on the heels of the highly damaging Walker spy ring and Pollard espionage cases. As **SA Alan Sipe** writes: The case began in 1986 and the Task Force (code name *Bobsled)* created to work this case was born in April 1987. **SA Lanny McCullah**, NCIS Headquarters FCI division head, understanding the complexity and high level spotlight, relocated to a space out of the NCIS Headquarters building and into a separate Washington DC office. Dozens of NCIS SAs came from near and far to work on this case. The Task Force ultimately included representatives from the Department of State, CIA, FBI and NSA, and grew to almost 100 personnel. The investigation resulted in arrest of four Marine Security Guards on a variety of charges and recall of 44 guards from nine US diplomatic stations. The Marine Corps prosecuted the cases. Lonetree was tried and found guilty of espionage and 12 other counts, and sentenced to 30 years in prison; his sentence was later reduced. After serving 8 years of his sentence he was released from prison in Fort Leavenworth, Kansas in 1996.

+ + + + + +

Wilfredo Garcia: **SA Jeff Norwitz** wrote about this espionage investigation. It developed from a larceny case when the suspect wanted to bargain by revealing spy activity of a fellow employee at the Mare Island Naval Shipyard in Vallejo, California. It ended with a successful prosecution in 1988. **Supervisor SA John Olson**, according to Norwitz, had seen his share of complex investigations in his thirty years of law enforcement, but this two year investigation topped the list! The following is an edited version of Norwitz' story.

Located 27 miles NE of San Francisco, Mare Island was a submarine construction and refit facility, and shipyard safes were full of submarine secrets. The larcenist turned cooperating witness (CW) advised that a navy sailor (Garcia) passed documents to the CW who copied them and arranged for them to be taken to Manila. The sailor had relatives in Manila who planned to sell them at the Soviet Embassy there. The case was complicated by the fact that Garcia's job as an investigator with Shipyard Investigations Branch gave him access to the entire industrial area.

The investigation included photo and video surveillance and court-ordered technical means of capturing Garcia's espionage-related activity at Mare Island. At the same time work was conducted by NCIS agents in Manila and Subic Bay. Initially, the plan was for NCIS agents in the Philippines to pose as foreign agents and buy the documents, but this plan failed. **SA Danny Fernandez** coordinated with the US Embassy and Philippine officials to obtain a search warrant for the residence of Garcia's relatives. Directed by SA Olson to do whatever was necessary to secure the classified information, NCIS agents and Philippine police entered the residence unannounced and *a near gun-battled broke out*. Nevertheless, the documents were recovered at this time. Back at Mare Island Garcia was interrogated by NCIS **SA Michael Lynch** and FBI SA Richard Hanf; they secured a signed admission so sound the defense stipulated to it at trial.

Garcia was sentenced to twelve years in prison in 1988. He was released in 1995 from a federal facility in Texas. Agents involved in this case at various levels in various places included three case agents and fourteen participating agents from nine offices in two countries and aboard an aircraft carrier.

DOUBLE AGENT OPERATIONS

[Author's Note: While NCIS investigations focus on stopping espionage already in progress, and prosecuting the spy, operations focus on trying to prevent spying. This is accomplished by giving foreign collectors someone actually controlled by NCIS. - thus the spy is actually a double agent. These operations require creativity, careful structure, and continuous training and review.]

OPERATION LEMONADE: In a joint NCIS / FBI operation beginning in 1977 Navy LCDR Art Lindberg, acting as a double agent, made an offer to sell information to the Soviets. He did this in a note he passed to an officer aboard a Soviet cruise ship operating out of New York City; the offer was accepted. During the course of this operation much was learned about Soviet espionage tradecraft and tactics. On May 20, 1978 three Soviet intelligence operatives were arrested. One (Zinyakin) had diplomatic immunity and was expelled from the US The other two Soviets (Chernayev and Enger) did not have immunity. They were convicted of espionage, sentenced to 50 years, and later traded for five Soviet dissidents in a swap at Kennedy Airport in New York. Various levels of operational management within NCIS included **SAs Vic Palmucci, Terry Tate,** and **Jack Parkey.** According to remarks written years ago by SA Palmucci, one side note is that SA Parkey testified in US District Court relative to his surveillance of the Soviets. He conducted this surveillance on the Garden State Parkway – on his motorcycle!

+ + + + + +

OPERATION SHOWDOWN: East German physicist and intelligence operative Alfred Zehe was arrested in Boston on November 3, 1983, while attending a science conference. This arrest came after a multi-year joint NCIS / FBI double agent operation using a civilian engineer employed by the navy as the double agent. Prosecuting this case was Robert Mueller, then a US Attorney in Boston and later Director of the FBI, and post-retirement appointed as a Special Counsel. *Zehe's conviction was a landmark in that all espionage activity occurred outside of the United States (whereas previous convictions were based on activity occurring inside the US).* Zehe was sentenced to four concurrent 8 year prison terms on April 4, 1985. In June of the same year he was part of an East-West spy swap conducted on the Ghenecke Bridge in Berlin. A Washington Post article states: *"The United States traded one accused spy and three convicted spies for 23 prisoners held in East German and Polish jails in what diplomats describe as the biggest East-West swap of its kind in Europe."* **SA Tricia Mansell** (author) was the NCIS Headquarters supervisor at the time of the arrest. Through the course of the operation many SAs were involved at various management levels, primarily those working in the NCIS Charleston, South Carolina office.

+ + + + + +

OPERATION STATION ZEBBRA: NCIS conducted an operation jointly with the Royal Canadian Mounted Police (RCMP) and the Canadian Security Intelligence Service (CSIS). Acting as the double agent was a female officer stationed at the US Naval Facility in Argentia, Newfoundland. The operation began aboard a Soviet Research Vessel in the harbor of St. Johns, Newfoundland in Dec 1986. Her handler was eventually identified as Stephen Ratkai, who held dual Canadian and Hungarian citizenship. Ratkai was arrested during a meeting with Geiger in June of 1988, and on 6 Feb 1989 he plead guilty to espionage in the Supreme Court of Newfoundland. He was sentenced to two concurrent nine year prison terms. *This marked the first conviction under Section 3 (1C) of the Canadian Official Secret Act for espionage.* Media reports after his release from prison he returned to Hungary.

+ + + + + +

1980s Double Agent Operations Personnel

Back row standing (l to r) SA Joe Hefferon, SA Mike Barrett, SA Wendell Tqguchi, Analyst Watson Pryor. Middle row kneeling (l to r) Secretary Little Tricia, SA Tricia Mansell, USMC LtCol Wayne Wildgrube, Supervisor SA Phil Comes. Front row kneeling: Petty Officer (?) and Secretary Evelyn.

+ + + + + +

The (possible ?) Spy that came in from the Cold: In a story written by retired Navy Reserve **CAPT Herman Hughes** in May 2013, CAPT Hughes details an incident occurring in Japan in 1968. What follows is a slightly edited version of this incident, in which he advises that at this time he was with NCIS in Atsugi, Japan, along with **SA Robert Foy.** Others aware of this incident were **SAs Anthony Perrin** and **Carl Sundstrom**.

"It was mid-winter and a near record snowstorm closed the base at Atsugi stranding many. SA Foy spent the night with me in my on-base quarters. Well after midnight I was awakened by phone and asked to go to the NCIS office. I woke SA FOY and we made it through the snow-filled streets to the office. Shortly after we arrived we got another phone call, this one from a US Navy Lieutenant who said he had an East German intelligence agent in tow who wanted to defect to the USA and was enroute from Tokyo to Atsugi by train. The LT had met the German at the East-West Discussion Group, a quasi-intellectual group with highly suspicious ties to North Korea and the USSR.

SA Foy and I contacted base transportation asking for a vehicle with snow chains. We were advised the only vehicle with chains was a pickup kept for use by the Command Duty Officer, who refused to allow us to borrow it. We commandeered the pickup, due to the national security implications, and drove to meet the LT and the East German. Since the pickup couldn't accommodate all of us the East German had to ride the short distance back to base in the bed of the truck; he was quite agitated by the time we arrived at the NCIS office.

SA Foy contacted the base hospital and asked for a medical doctor; when the doctor arrived he said he didn't want to get involved and left. The East German was then supplied with some liquor which calmed him down considerably. He then said he was in fear of his life. He said he was actually a White Russian by birth and a Soviet intelligence agent undercover in Tokyo posing as a newspaper reporter from West Berlin. He said his son had been killed, reportedly in a hit-and-run accident, but he did not believe it was an accident and he was worried that further harm would befall his family.

Not knowing what to believe I felt it was necessary to get him to someone higher up the food chain so I contacted a former colleague with ties to the CIA. The Atusgi base commander provided us with a helicopter on which SA Foy and another NCIS agent accompanied this man to Fuchu Air Base. NCIS SAs were not allowed to be a part of the ensuing CIA interrogation, and later that day SA Foy was contacted by higher authorities and told not to make any written report of this incident – but rather, *treat it like it never happened*. As far as we know nothing official has ever been written about this incident; we are left to speculate what did or didn't happen to this man."

The Spy that came in from the Cold – and left! Based on information in media and provided by retired **SA Joseph Riccio**, what follows is a summary of the shadows and mysteries involving the defection and re-defection of Soviet KGB agent Vitaly Yurchenko. Known within the intelligence community is that motivations and mindsets of spies vary: Ideology, monetary gain, fame (as in a chance to be important), love, perhaps even having a martyr complex may motivate one to the act of spying. Maybe Yurchenko is the only one who knows for sure who he really is, what happened, and why he did what he did . . . . . the debate continues.

What many people don't know is that KGB agent Vitaly Yurchenko defected to the United States during the timeframe he came

103

from Moscow to Rome to meet with an NCIS double agent. A tangled plot to be sure!

Yurchenko contacted the US Embassy in Rome on August 1, 1985 asking to defect. He was flown to Washington D.C. for debriefings. Three months later Yurchenko was eating in a Georgetown restaurant accompanied by a CIA officer, and he simply walked out of the restaurant, found his way to the Soviet Embassy, and went back to Moscow, re-defecting. Was this a true re-defection; a change of mind on the part of Yurchenko? Was this a KGB operation structured to task Yurchenko to obtain as much insight as possible on the way the US handled defectors, including what their priorities were in intelligence collection, and then come home? The world of espionage is always complicated, but this defection was more complicated than most. Yurchenko's defection was in the middle of a NCIS double agent operation.

The double agent was a Navy Chief assigned to the US Naval Communications Center in Naples. His Soviet handler was KGB agent Aleksandr Mikhailovich Chepil, known to the Chief as Alex. The Chief met with Alex for about two years, receiving money and tasking and in return providing materials to maintain the interest of the Soviets. On their last meeting Alex brought with him Yurchenko, who proceeded to question the Chief deeply about his job and access to information. Three days later Yurchenko defected.

To further complicate the mystery, multiple media has reported that Yurchenko, though married in Moscow, was in love with a Russian woman married to either a diplomat or a Soviet trade official working in Canada. Yurchenko may or may not have flown secretly to Canada to meet with her and she may or may not have been the Soviet woman who committed suicide by jumping from a high balcony in October

1985. Perhaps he had hopes for something there that didn't materialize – or, perhaps none of this reporting is valid.

NCIS agents working this matter include, but may not be limited to: **SAs Joe Hefferon, Joseph Riccio, Ron Olive, Bill Nugent**, and **Brent Barrett**.

+ + + + + +

[Author's Note: What follows are more recent espionage investigations compiled from open media sources as identified. They are included here as examples of continuing collection efforts by adversaries of the US.]

PEOPLE'S REPUBLIC OF CHINA: One example in a case involving NCIS: Chi Mak passed classified technology to the Chinese possibly as early as 1988 until his arrest and prosecution in 2007.

In a joint FBI / NCIS investigation exposing the Chinese in stealing US secrets, spy Chi Mak (believed to be a trained operative emigrating from Hong Kong and actually planted in the US by Chinese intelligence) was uncovered. Beginning in 1988 Mak worked for a California company named Power Paragon which developed power systems for the US Navy.

Through surveillance, recordings, and searches it was learned that Mak was tasked to collect a wide variety of military technology information, and his younger brother Tai Mak and Tai's wife Fuk were involved in transporting this information back to China. The investigation started around 2004 and culminated in arrest and then a six week jury trial in May 2007.

Mak was convicted and sentenced to 24 and ½ years, Tai plead guilty and was sentenced to 10 years, Mak's wife spent 3 years in prison and was then was deported to China, Tai's wife and son were deported to China. Mentioned prominently in the article was **NCIS SA Gunnar Newquist**. *Source: The New Yorker May 12, 2014 by Yudhijit Bhattacharjee*

+ + + + + +

RUSSIAN FEDERATION: Retired Petty Officer First Class (PO1) submarine sailor Robert Hoffman was attempting to provide highly classified information to Russia. This joint FBI / NCIS investigation was triggered in 2011 when PO1 Hoffman, nearing retirement, told friends he planned a trip to Belarus; all about this trip seemed suspicious to many. Subsequently Hoffman delivered classified information to operatives he believed to be working for Russian intelligence.

He was arrested and found guilty in a jury trial in Norfolk, Virginia in August 2013. At this time he was 40 years old. He was sentenced to 40 years in prison.

Source: 03/07/2014 https://www.fbi.gov/news/stories/2014/march/naval-espionage-stopping-a-dangerous-insider-threat/naval-espionage-stopping-a-dangerous-insider-threat

+ + + + + +

MIDDLE EAST: This case involves the arrest of a man born in Saudi Arabia named Mostafa Ahmed Awwad, of Muslim faith, married in 2007 in Cairo to a US citizen, who then moved to the US in 2012 and became a US citizen. He worked at the Norfolk Naval Shipyard as an engineer.

In a joint FBI/NCIS investigation Awwad was arrested in December 2014 and in 2015 plead guilty to attempted espionage. He was sentenced to 11 years in prison. His goal was to utilize his position with the US Navy to obtain military technology for use by the

Egyptian government, including but not limited to the designs of the USS Gerald R. Ford nuclear aircraft carrier, a new Navy 'supercarrier.

NCIS SA Susan Triesch is quoted as saying: *"This case demonstrates that NCIS aggressively pursues anyone who would endanger our national security by targeting critical platforms like the Ford class carrier. The close collaboration between NCIS and the FBI thwarted this insider threat and we will continue cooperative efforts to safeguard those who protect and serve in the Department of the Navy."* Source: June 18, 2015 http://www.examiner.com/article/ncis-saudi-engineer-attempts-to-steal-u-s-aircraft-carrier-plans-schematics

Chapter 7: **Places**

NCIS Keflavik, Iceland

SA Bob Powers wrote an extensive history of the NCIS office in Iceland, which opened in 1964 and closed in 2002. He noted that counterintelligence was the main mission of NCIS Keflavik, which had a large Communist Party in the 1960s and 1970s. In the late 1960s, the Soviet Embassy in Reykjavik was one of the Soviet's largest, with 87 members of their delegation to Iceland identified as KGB or GRU. Because the airport was combined military and civilian they were allowed mostly unrestricted access. The Marines who stood guard were provided with the license numbers of automobiles used by KGB or GRU, and they called NCIS so we could monitor these Soviets while they were on the base.

NCIS Keflavik had a vintage Quonset hut, located in the industrial area of the base. It was used in several capacities; one of which was a safe house. In the winter of 1975 **SA Larry Ferrell** drove by the safe house on the way home and noticed a light on and someone moving inside. No one was supposed to be there, and this hut had been subject to burglaries, so SA Ferrell called Navy Security for support. Two patrol officers showed up, kicked the door off its hinges and rushed in yelling *"Freeze"*. They threw the intruder against the wall and handcuffed him. When the intruder was turned around Larry recognized him as the Assistant Supervising Agent from NCIS London, **SA Bob Kain**. SA Kain had made travel arrangements with **SA George Morse**, who had neglected to notify NCIS Keflavik!

During **SA Darryl Toler's** assignment in October 1986, President Ronald Reagan and Soviet Prime Minister Mikhail Gorbachev met in Reykjavik. NCIS Keflavik, augmented by NCIS Norfolk, played a significant part in PSD's for both men, especially since their arrivals and departures were at the airport in Keflavik.

The flag of Iceland was raised and the flag of the US was lowered, as the US handed over the Naval Air Station to the Government of Iceland on 8 September 2006. NAS Keflavik's last commanding officer, CAPT Mark S. Laughton, presided over a ceremony effecting the disestablishment of the air station.

+ + + + + +

NCIS New York

Former Director J. Brian McKee was a native New Yorker who spent many years with NCIS in and around New York as a young agent, a Supervisor, and a Regional Director with NCIS. He wrote an article in the fall of 2011 in which he discusses liaison through the years between NCIS and the New York Police Department (NYPD). Salient points of this article address the NCIS involvement in PSDs in New York, the *Fleet Week* hosted each year by New York, and the NCIS espionage and criminal investigations conducted in this city.

SA McKee describes NYPD as having well over 35,000 personnel as well as a small Air Force and Navy. He notes NCIS has limited presence in the area and through the years have sought support from NYPD, and have soundly received this support,

For PSDs, NYPD has assisted by using boats, helicopters, hundreds of police, whatever has been needed as NCIS protects the many navy affiliated dignitaries passing through this city. Director McKee states, "**SA Paul Sparks** still holds the record of being responsible for the only time that all 24 lanes of traffic in Times Square was momentarily halted by NYPD officers to permit safe passage of an NCIS motorcade from the West side to the East side of Manhattan."

In 1976 New York City hosted the bicentennial of 1776 with a huge international Naval Review involving warships from many world countries. For security purposes NCIS sent over 100 agents to work with hundreds of NYPD officers out of a command center at NYPD Headquarters. NCIS requested a police supervisor with military experience to lead this event, and Ray Kelly was selected. Otherwise known as **LtCol Kelly,** he was in the USMC reserves, and recalled to active duty for two weeks to lead this event. Director McKee notes this "went down in the history of the NYPD as the most successful major security event."

Director McKee also states long before arrest authority was addressed nationwide, NYPD and the New York court system fully recognized NCIS Special Agents as police officers. NCIS worked diligently to maintain good relationships with all levels of NYPD leadership, and it fostered a uniquely wonderful partnership.

SA Joe Orrigo speaks warmly of his first NCIS assignment, which was at NCIS New York: "I was a SA assigned to the New York Resident Agency located at the Brooklyn Navy Yard. . . Responsibility, thoroughness and reputation were the key aspects of the job . . .

camaraderie among the agents was critical as were unofficial mentors . . . two of the very best were NCIS **SA Vinny Giame** and **SA Terry Olson.**"

NCIS North Island, California

SA Tricia Mansel/ (author) was assigned as an agent at NCIS North Island during the late 1970s and early 1980s, and writes: "It always surprised me when agents assigned elsewhere considered NCIS North Island to be a somewhat sleepy assignment; in fact, it was anything but that. Aircraft carriers and large cruisers were home ported there, aviation squadrons included helicopters and anti-submarine warfare planes, a large naval air rework facility and a defense property disposal office were on base, as was COMNAVAIRPAC. Under us was an office at Coronado where SEALS trained, dolphins were trained, various small boat units were located, as well as a Surface Warfare Office School and COMNAVSURFPAC. Also, the navy operations based on San Clemente Island were under NCIS North Island. Being the agent on duty almost always meant working through the night or weekend. One of my supervisors was **SA Ted Miller**, who was back for a second tour during my tenure there. His first tour at North Island was in the early 1970s.

While a SA at North Island I worked a joint NCIS / Chula Vista PD bigamy case involving a navy sailor who worked on base and lived in neighboring Chula Vista. It led to a successful prosecution, but the details were nothing like the ones in a case **SA Ted Miller** worked in the early '70s. His bigamy case had unbelievable parameters that garnered widespread media coverage at the conclusion. "

In summary, **SA Miller's case:** A baby boy was born to Michael and Rebecca Slater on December 11, 1947. This baby was put up for adoption and became the son of Mr. and Mrs. Kitzmiller who named him Wyley; he grew up and joined the navy.

Michael Slater (the biological father) went to extensive lengths to track and photograph Wyley, through the years and at a distance. He eventually introduced himself. Michael then introduced his wife (and Wyley's biological mother) Rebecca to Wyley.

In very short order Wyley Kitzmiller fell in love with, married, and had a child with his natural mother. The case was worked by NCIS jointly with local law enforcement. In the fall of 1971 **SAs Ted Miller** and **Ed Fitzpatrick**, along with San Diego Detective Johnny Williams, boarded the *USS Chicago (CG 11)* while it was still underway entering port. SA Miller remembers "*t*o say the least it was a bit dicey climbing up the accommodation ladder to board this mighty warship".

Sailor Wyley was detained onboard; eventually he and his wife / mother were prosecuted for felony bigamy and both received jail sentences. During a search of Kitzmiller's residence, weapons and notes were found indicating Kitzmiller had researched ways to *kill his natural father.*

As a Special Agent Afloat aboard the *USS Ticonderoga (CV 14)* **SA Ted Miller** was able to observe the splashdown and retrieval of the crew on Apollo 17. These men were the last humans to walk on the moon, using a land rover to cover great distances in order to collect lunar soil and rock samples. It was on this same deployment SA Miller crossed the equator and went from a pollywog to shellback in a time-honored naval tradition. He can still feel the sting of those fire hose paddles he recounts. Like most who have been through this ceremony, he will never forget it.

+ + + + + +

NCIS Okinawa

SA Toni Perrin writes that he arrived NCIS Okinawa in the summer of 1968; it was his first office as an SRA. The office was located at Naha Air Force Base at the southern end of the island in two

Quonset Huts. The problem was 80% of the work then was in northern Okinawa at Camps Courtney, Hansen, and Schwab. It took two hours to drive from Naha to Camp Schwab, and NCIS Okinawa had junk vehicles requisitioned from the Defense Property Disposal Office with over 200,000 miles on them.

SA Perrin recalls: "My NCIS Okinawa experience was really the most significant assignment I had in my career, simply because of the complexities of the time and the growth of the office." The growth came when the battling for jurisdiction between NCIS and USMC CID stopped, and NCIS received all the cases within their legal jurisdiction. SA Perrin states that when he arrived in Okinawa, he was given one permanent agent to work with and one agent on temporary duty. After he left, the office was beefed up to 18 agents and then about 30 agents. "But we were the pioneers," he stated. "Some of those pioneers were **SAs Blair Gluba, Laddie Hancock, Charlie Richter, John Walsh, Tommy Williams, Dale Townsend, Jim Bauer,** and **Mike Kuhar**."

SA Perrin said the caseload quickly ballooned, agents were working up to 80 hours a week, no one was ever in the office except to drop off reports they had taken home to write. "Agents were on the road all day. No one would answer radio calls from me as they knew I would give them another case. We had one case where a disgruntled Marine walked into the First Sergeant's office and shot him in the chest. I got the call within minutes. I put out a call to 'any Okinawa agents' and got no response. When I broadcast that the First Sergeant had been shot, four guys answered up!" Because of limited housing new agents arrived unaccompanied, got on a housing list, and it was six months to a year before their families could arrive.

In terms of the office, NCIS scouted for a new office up north and got an empty building on Camp Courtney. The agents made a do-it

-yourself move over the weekend, hauling all our furniture, safes, etc. in borrowed military trucks. "We started moving on a Friday and were operating on Monday from Camp Courtney."

When the Division came back, NCIS was ordered out of their spaces by the Commanding General, General Louis Wilson, future Commandant and Medal of Honor recipient. SA Perrin says, "He did not suffer fools well. The first week the Division was back, they had a break-in of their armory at Camp Hansen. The crooks got three M-60 machine guns and fifty 45 caliber pistols. General Wilson was LIVID. In three days, we had all of the weapons recovered and three Marines in the brig." SA Perrin then got a call from the Camp Commander. He said, *"Toni, the General says we're going to need you guys more than we need the spaces. You can stay."*

+ + + + + +

NCIS Pensacola, Florida

SA George McClellan writes: In late 1975, I was transferred from the Philippines to NCIS Pensacola, Florida. Upon arrival I was informed that I would be the Special Agent Afloat on the *USS Lexington (CVT 16)*, the Navy's at-sea training carrier. I spent fourteen great productive months aboard this vessel, had a Commander's stateroom across the passage from the Officers Mess and two hatches down from the ship's Executive Officer. I was there when the movie "Midway" was filmed and for the first visit since WWII of a Soviet Naval Delegation aboard a US Navy Aircraft Carrier. They were involved in a Law of the Sea's conference held in New Orleans.

But, this article is focused on what happened at NCIS Pensacola after I left the carrier. NCIS moved into a reconditioned building to be solely occupied by NCIS. I was given an office on the far end next to a door that led directly to the outside. The supervisor, **SA Lee Miller,** thought it would be easier for informants to come in by a back door to see me. (It was expected that I would start developing plans to protect NAS Pensacola from criminals, spies, terrorists and the like, as I had successfully used informants in operations in the Philippines.)

In 1977, on a Saturday afternoon when I was in the office performing my turn as a duty agent, in walked a Petty Officer who wanted to chat. He possessed a State of Florida Scrap Iron Dealers license and had a lucrative side business collecting and selling scrap metal. He told me he had been approached by two civilian employees of the Naval Air Rework Facility (NARF) with a proposition to fence Navy scrap metal; they were new to Florida and didn't know how to get rid of it.

These civilians showed the Petty Officer a large pile of scrap metal, upon which he saw a brand new rotor shaft for a helicopter. Thus was the start of an operation that lasted nearly a year. Of course the FBI were notified of the *Theft on a Government Reservation* crime and said they would probably assume investigative jurisdiction. But, I learned from my old Supervising Agent, SA Sherm Bliss, *"NCIS investigation will continue until the FBI darkens your door"*.

It was several days before an FBI agent came by; he was a new agent and keen to be involved so we worked a joint operation. Eventually he was very helpful in coming up with the $6,000 to pay the two civilians for a purchase by our informant. The property stolen was basically avionics such as transponders, radios, and radars. Also the stolen property included landing gear and, of course, rotor shafts. I provided our informant with a navy van for moving the stolen property

116

off NAS Pensacola to an unused but NCIS-secured hanger at NAS Whiting Field, where it was stored, inventoried, and photographed.

At the end of the operation, when the payoff was made, the two civilians (with the cash) disappeared into the NARF hanger before anybody could see where they went. The young FBI agent nearly had a heart attack. The cash was found, eventually, stuffed in the insulation inside the cockpit of an F4 trainer. The two men arrested were Navy civilian employees who had accepted transfer to NARF Pensacola when the Navy closed a similar facility in New Jersey. The FBI also said the two were low level soldiers in a Mafia family trying to make a name.

We recovered over $100K in stolen Navy goods; not too bad for a criminal investigative agency turning from reactive to proactive in crime fighting.

+ + + + + +

NCIS Sigonella, Sicily

The following extracts are from an article written by **SA John Olson** describing arriving with his family for a tour in Sicily and being met by the family of sponsor **SA Al Zane**. "The Zane's assured the Olson's that a trench had been dug so that lava from Mt. Etna would flow down the other side. . . .NCIS Sigonella is located aboard the Naval Air Facility on a plain near the seaport of Catania. The families of SAs assigned there live on Mt. Etna in lava pits. . . . The Olson's villa is in the middle of a mid-1800 lava flow; one can still see the roof of an old farmhouse across the road buried in this eruption. The Zane's live in a lava flow dating back to 1669. . . . During the winter it can snow on Mt. Etna . . . Children must be bussed down the hill to a school located aboard base. . . Wine is (best bought at the package store on base, otherwise) it comes from a drive-in vino place. Bring an empty bottle or jug, drive up to the pump, and just like a gas pump, fill 'er up!" SA Olson advises that the Zane's and Olson's witnessed close hand a major eruption (grandest in 50 years) and the lava did flow down the other side of the mountain. Also, "water ceased to flow in our Casa's, our yards and laundry were black and our bodies were grey, but we made it and have pictures to prove it."

+ + + + + +

SINGAPORE: Southeast Asia Field Office

Former Supervisor in Singapore, **SA Greg Bachman**, writes: **SA Mike Hickman** was assigned to Singapore in 1991, and in 1992 the office moved from downtown into the building it still occupies at the Port of Singapore Authority Sembawang Wharves on the northern tip of the island. Also in 1992, NCIS hired retired US Navy Senior Chief Yeoman Terry Leggett, who would shepherd the administrative aspects of this office for the next 17 years. In 2005 Singapore became the Southeast Asia Field Office, covering 26 countries from India to the East and New Zealand to the west. SA Bachman advises that the bulk of the work is "counterintelligence support to Force Protection" to mitigate threats against Navy and DOD asset.

SA Neill Robbins contributed the following information: **SAs John Morgan** and **John Cusack,** brought to our attention the current home page of the *Singapore Central Narcotics Bureau* (cnb.gov.sg) which depicts several photos, the attached being one of them. Of interest is the fact that this photo was captured in 1973 after an out-country drug suppression operation involving the NCIS *Scoutmaster/ Stable Boy* program. John Morgan provided the 'original' of that photo and if you look closely, you can see **SAs John Morgan**, **Bobby Brady**, and **John Cusack**.

The photo was taken at the Mayflower Hotel at the end of the operation. Keeping in mind this occurred close to 50 years ago, John Cusack advised it was a *Scoutmaster / Stable Boy* operation run by

NCIS Philippines (83PS) which followed an earlier operation in Hong Kong worked by **SAs John Marquette** and **John Roberts**.

John advised that John Morgan arrived in Singapore first and worked with CNB for a couple of days until Brady and Cusack and the three informants arrived aboard the *USS Constellation (CV-64)* from Subic. **Kirby Sumner** was the Agent afloat and helped during the operation which ended when the *USS Constellation* departed Singapore. According to John, the CNB folks were very professional and pleased with the timing of their arrival as a new narcotics law had recently been passed and the operation gave them a greater opportunity to apply it.

Not only is this just downright unreal all these years later, but it speaks to the impact that the *Scoutmaster / Stable Boy* program had assisting Seventh Fleet assets deal with the significant drug problems back in the 1970's.

+ + + + + +

Republic of the Philippines: NCIS Subic Bay

SA John Morgan writes about his observations of the area when assigned there in the early 1970's. Subic Bay was the largest naval installation in that part of the Pacific, covering a land mass of 152 square miles and including repair, supply, and a number of Naval and Marine Corps installations. Close by was Cubi Point Naval Air Station with massive runways and piers to accommodate carriers and their air wings.

Olongapo, the town outside of the main gate, was a place where 2 million sailors and marines descended annually; the town was full of booze, girls, and drugs. There were about two miles of bars and brothels interspersed with restaurants and shops. The most common form of transportation was by Jeepney. *[Aiuthor's note: Having been there in the 1970s myself, I can add that it was an area of poverty and desperation where the local populace mostly depended on US military to pour money into their economy. For a beautiful location, if able to get the time off, many military traveled about 100 miles to the beautiful resort of Baguio.]*

+ + + + + +

Kodiak Island, Alaska 1966

The following are excerpts from an article written in 1966 by **SA Fred Robey**: "Large island (the size of Connecticut) . . . magnificent scenery . . . schools of dolphin frolic . . . a whale occasionally passes by. Population in 1960 was about 2,500 in a sleepy little fishing village, population grew to 7,000 by 1966 due to increase at Naval Base and expansion of fishing industry. People are friendly and civic minded . . . television and radio are one station each broadcast by Naval Base . . . two restaurants and one small theater. It is considered a 'banana belt' in the North Pacific, with thick green foliage in the summer that turn to shrubs in the winter."

+ + + + + +

GUAM

SA Anthony Perrin writes of one case involving NCIS and the death of a DEA Agent, and another event involving the fall of Saigon.

"On December 19, 1975 Larry D. Wallace, 32 years old and a Drug Enforcement Administration (DEA) agent, died at the Naval Regional Medical Center in Guam from gunshot wounds received during an undercover drug investigation. SA Wallace was assigned to the Tokyo

District Office of DEA, but in Guam working against a group of heroin traffickers. NCIS SA Stan White was near the scene when a drug buy went bad. While in a parking lot the suspect (Francisco Guerrero) advised the heroin was stored a few minutes away. Guerrero was handcuffed and placed in a vehicle with DEA SA Wallace and his partner, DEA SA Frank Quintal. Guerrero managed to retrieve a concealed .38 caliber handgun and shot SA Quintal twice; the second bullet went through Quintal's arm and struck SA Wallace in the head. The vehicle crashed, SA Stan White ran over, stuck his gun in Guerrero's face and said, *"Drop your gun or I will blow your brains out!"* Guerrero dropped his gun."

SA Toni Perrin was a back-up nearby. He recalls telephoning the DEA office in the Philippines to advise that one DEA SA was dead and another was in the hospital. "It was a truly sad day to say the least," SA Perrin says. "Suspect Guerrero was convicted and got a life sentence. They brought a special US Attorney out from San Diego to try the case."

Late April 1975 was the *fall of Saigon* in the Vietnamese war. Admiral G. Steve Morrison was the Commander, Naval Marianas at the time. ADM Morrison got a call from the Commander-in-Chief, Pacific Fleet who told him to prepare to receive and house up to 150 thousand refugees; the first plane load would arrive Guam in three hours. In turn, NCIS Guam got a call from ADM Morrison. It was a logistical nightmare but the navy pulled it off. Refugee camps were set up with tents on an abandoned airstrip on base; NCIS came up with a plan to police and monitor the refugee camps.

In recalling this story, **SA Perrin** also mentioned Admiral Morrison was the father of Jim Morrison, the legendary rock star and lead singer for the DOORS, a chart-topping band of the era. [*Author's note: Multiple media sources report that the two had become* *estranged before Jim Morrison died. Jim Morrison's gravesite - in Paris - is one of the most visited in the world.*]

+ + + + + +

NCIS HEADQUARTERS

Records indicate that on or about mid-July 1969 NCIS HQ moved to the 8th, 9th, and 10th floors of the Hoffman Building at 301 Taylor Drive, Alexandria, Virginia. The building is located along Interstate Highway 495 just west of the Woodrow Wilson Bridge connecting Maryland and Virginia. Following this, NCIS HQ moved to Suitland, Maryland, then to the Washington Navy Yard. In 2011 NCIS HQ moved to the Russell-Knox Building at 27130 Telegraph Road, Quantico, Virginia 22554. This same building is also the Headquarters for the Air Force Office of Special Investigations, the Defense Intelligence Agency, the Defense Security Service, and the United States Army Criminal Investigation Command.

The Base Realignment and Consolidation (BRAC) committee recommended the consolidation of NCIS HQ and other military HQ counterparts into one building; a site in Quantico, Virginia was selected. Following an agency-wide request for suggestions to name the newly constructed building, **NCIS SA Tricia Mansell** (author) submitted the name *Russell-Knox Building*. [*Author's Note: My rationale for this name was simple: I thought the name should be a combination of one Marine and one Navy man, each of whom was involved in the roots of NCIS (which came from early ONI). These men were General John H. Russell and Commodore Dudley Wright Knox. Both are buried in Arlington National Cemetery, Virginia.*]

General Russell, a United States Naval Academy (USNA) graduate, had an exemplary career including duty with ONI from

1913-1917. He was appointed Commandant of the Marine Corps in 1934. Commodore Knox also graduated from the USNA and had an exemplary career. He served in ONI from 1914 to 1916, crossing paths with General Russell. He was a gold medal essayist with the Naval Institute, an editor of military publications, and a keeper, writer and curator of naval history in various capacities.

Russell-Knox Building (RKB)

Ft. Leavenworth, Kansas

Where do convicted felons in NCIS investigations go to prison? There are dozens of brigs and federal prisons spread throughout the country; some are mentioned in this book. These range from low to high security and criminals are placed according to crime, location, and inmate population.

Ft. Leavenworth in Kansas is one prison often heard in the military community, and indeed it has a history. It is the oldest penal institution in continuous operation in the Federal system. Operations started in May 1875 at this US Military Prison and continue today. It is now officially called the US Disciplinary Barracks, and nicknamed *The Castle*. It houses about 1,450 men sent there from all military branches and bases throughout the world. It is a massive stone building with eight wings radiating from a central six-story rotunda. *(Sources: http://articles.latimes.com/1988-12-04/news/mn-1341_1_military-discipline ; http://usdb.leavenworth.army.mil/main.htm)*

Ft. Leavenworth

Chapter 8: **SPECIAL AGENT AFLOAT (SAA) PROGRAM**

In 1967 SAs were assigned from NCIS Europe on a thirty day rotational basis in support of Sixth Fleet aircraft carriers. This was in response to an apparent need for more sophisticated methods of criminal investigation on deployed warships. The first SA assigned for a full deployment was in 1971, and thereafter SAs have been assigned tours to include deployments and/or as day agents while carriers are at their homeport.

In a 1970s article by **SA Ken Anthony**, he called being a Special Agent Afloat (SAA) "the ultimate in NCIS independent duty" providing the opportunity for a SA to "resolve complex cases . . . meet with Admirals and other dignitaries . . . build a level of confidence that will last a career . . . and make memorable personal experiences which might include visiting foreign ports, hi-lining between ships at sea, catapulting off the deck of an aircraft carrier, and dropping in on a destroyer via a line from a helicopter."

One of the SAA stories begins with the NCIS office in Beirut, Lebanon. NCIS established an office in Beirut in early 1983 under the control of the office in Naples, Italy. This was a time of extreme conflict within Lebanon; in fact a Civil War was raging. With USN and USMC assets in the area it was obvious NCIS needed a presence. **SA John D'Avanzo,** in charge of the NCIS Naples office, traveled to Beirut to assess the situation. He made the choice of positioning the Beirut office aboard a ship, rather than the alternate location of the Marine Barracks, which proved to be fateful. One NCIS agent became known as the *phantom* agent in Beirut because he flew in and out to assist the assigned agent and to work among the locals developing important contacts. This was **SA Eddie Hemphill**. The other four agents assigned there, in successive order, were **SAs Walter Foch, Ray Carman, Grant McIntosh, and Rod Staudinger.** It was **SA McIntosh** who was there, aboard ship, when a truck loaded with explosives made its way into the inner atrium of the barracks; the explosion killed 220 Marines, 16 Navy, and 3 Army personnel. The date was October 23, 1983.

One of the Navy men killed was Michael Gorchinski, a Chief Electronics Technician from the battleship *USS New Jersey* (BB 62)

anchored offshore Beirut. He had gone ashore to assist the marines with work on their radar equipment.

Later, on just one single day (Feb 08, 1984) the USS New Jersey fired almost 300 shells at Druze and Syrian positions in the Bekaa Valley east of Beirut. Multiple naval history sources report this was the heaviest shore bombardment since the Korean War. The *USS New Jersey* deployment extended to eleven months, which was one of the longest in naval history.

It is safe to say that NCIS SAs must be flexible, adventurous, prepared for whatever serves the needs of the Navy and Marine Corps, and nothing showcases this better than agents deployed at sea or forward deployed to battle environments.

+ + + + + +

SA Gordon Crossman worked for ONI / NCIS from 1963 to 1986. In 1972 and 1973 he served as the Special Agent Afloat aboard the *USS Forrestal (CV-59)*. For his many achievements he was awarded the Meritorious Civil Service Award. He has written an article summarizing his experiences, and what follows are extracts, in his own words, of his time serving aboard this ship:

"In July 1972 I had the privilege of being the first SAA to be assigned to the USS Forrestal (CVA-59). Our carrier was like a small city of 5000 people and eighty aircraft, where personnel worked in shifts twenty four hours a day. Some individuals were eating breakfast while others were having dinner.

When I reported aboard it was a time of great turbulence, for the ship had just been crippled by a maliciously induced fire. And, it was a difficult time as many young marines and sailors were against the war in Vietnam and did not want to be in the military. It was a time when our ships needed to be protected from the crew as well as the enemy.

The destruction of government property, damage to the ships' infrastructure, racial problems, and the use of illegal drugs, were the major problems. To make matters worse some sailor distributed an underground newsletter targeting the SAA, which included informing the reader what to do should he be interviewed or interrogated by me. During my deployment I visited fifteen other ships in company with the USS Forrestal to conduct investigations as well as training for their security forces. I would fly by helicopter to other ships at sea and descend on a rope onto the fantail of the ship while it was underway. When I finished, the helicopter would return and pick me up the same way they let me down.

Everyone aboard the carrier had an assigned battle station except for me, so when the battle station alarm was sounded I could stay in my stateroom or go to the ship's wardroom. The Commanding Officer gave me one standing order: I was to call the bridge immediately if someone was reported overboard. He was very concerned for my safety because of my activities aboard ship.

I often used disguises as I moved about the Forrestal at night by obtaining department T-Shirts and wearing the ship's baseball cap. Each department had different colored T-shirts (white, green, yellow, red, purple), which identified their respective duties. This made it possible to walk up on individuals committing criminal acts, since they ignored individuals wearing their colors. During this SAA assignment I conducted over 250 investigations and prepared thirty five informational reports on counterintelligence matters, including several port studies. And I used the ship's closed circuit TV to brief the crew prior to port calls. "

+ + + + + +

[*Author's note: SAs deployed have good reason to be cautious. Anyone who has ever worked aboard a carrier understands the danger involved in everyday operations, where one can easily get lost, get swept off the flight deck, bang everything on your body with the steel ladders and knee knocker doorways, etc.. Not to mention that, as the most senior 'lawman' aboard, one can have a target on your back, and so can those with whom one has any association. See below story.*]

The following is a summary of an article written years ago by **SA Raymond Blackwell** about a July 2, 1979, murder aboard an East Coast aircraft carrier. The carrier was conducting local operations off the coast in the Atlantic Ocean. Two sailors eventually plead guilty to murder at their respective Court Martials and each was sentenced to life imprisonment. Together they had used an oar to beat another sailor to death and then thrown his body overboard. The victim was actually a subject of an ongoing investigation and had been in the NCIS SA's stateroom for questioning at least three times. The suspects mistook seeing him there as evidence that he was a *Narc*, thus the motive for the murder. The victim never worked with the NCIS SA or the ship MAAs. His body was never recovered. Crime scene examination revealed blood splatter, and a sailor came forward to report witnessing this murder, thus the conviction.

In 1986 **SA Tom Fischer** was appointed as the first NCIS Special Agent Afloat Program Manager. SA Fisher had served as a SAA aboard the *USS Dwight D. Eisenhower (CVN-69)* from January 1980 to January 1981. SA Fisher discusses the demands of being an agent afloat and advises such an agent must possess "good judgment, professional competency, tact, confidence, flexibility, and have the

131

ability to function independently in making decisions and interfacing with senior Navy Officers."

+ + + + + +

SA Bob Robbins wrote about his time as the first SAA on the *USS Enterprise (CVAN-65)*: "I arrived at NCIS Alameda just days before deployment, found no supplies for me aboard the ship, so was greatly assisted by SA Earl Johnson and other NCIS agents in Alameda and San Francisco in stocking up for the deployment: common office supplies, investigative forms, crime scene kit items, and a copy of NIS-1 and NIS-2.

After a *fast transit* from San Francisco, the USS Enterprise arrived in Subic Bay. I went ashore to report to the NCIS supervisor, and drawing only on my previous CONUS experiences, I reported to the office in a suit and tie. This was probably the first time anyone had seen a SA in a coat and tie in ages.

I was welcomed by everyone, especially supervisor **SA Jimmy Jones**. The support I received from him and **SA Dave Kerr** was invaluable.

After leaving Subic bay, I settled into my role as the SA assigned to the ship. I had the support of the CO and the XO, and was consulted on all issues regarding security and investigations. I worked closely with the Chief Master-at-Arms and with the Legal Officer regarding any issues involving investigations or security.

Personal Note: My ability to relate to the ship and task force (CTF-77) staff was greatly enhanced by my prior naval service and completion of the Naval Aviation Officer training program at Pensacola, FL. My aviation training certainly helped when I utilized helicopter transport between ships in the Tonkin Gulf. Knowing my training and prior experience as an Air Intelligence Officer and photo-intelligence analyst, I was asked by the Executive Officer if I would be willing to occasionally assist as a reserve officer in the intelligence center if needed to help with photo analysis and strike planning. I agreed to do so, only if there was no conflict with my Special Agent Afloat duties. Although I was not called on to perform such duties, I frequently visited the Intelligence Operations Center to refresh my skills to be prepared if I was called on. The USS Enterprise awarded me an unsolicited Vietnam Service Medal for my service as a Reserve Officer and my military service record was updated to reflect Vietnam service.

Most of my daily activities aboard the *USS Enterprise* were related to criminal investigations involving drug abuse, thefts, and assaults. I vividly recall one case, in which I recruited an informant to purchase LSD from a suspect. The suspect, at the time of the controlled transfer, was an Aviation Ordnance man working at night on the fight deck loading explosive ordnance. When apprehended, he advanced towards me swinging a tie-down chain and threatening to kill me. After advising him (using more direct language that I will now admit) that I was prepared to use *lethal force* (my issued revolver) he fortunately dropped the tie-down chain and surrendered. Following the seizure of over 600 hits of LSD from his person, he was transferred to NAS Subic bay for processing and court martial."

A sample of SA Robbins further recollections:

"During a port call in Hong Kong, I went ashore with the advance party and established liaison contact with a British Colonial Police officer named Trevor Howard. Once the USS Enterprise arrived in port, I accompanied Detective Constable Howard on an evening tour of establishments that were considered *trouble spots* frequently visited by US sailors. While in one such establishment I overheard a comment from several sailors, "Let's throw those guys out of OUR bar". I became somewhat concerned about a possible fight, when Constable Howard said, *"No worries Mate"* and withdrew a Webley .455 revolver from under his shirt and placed it on the bar without saying a word. The rumblings from the US Sailors in the bar immediately ceased and we finished our drinks and left. I returned to the ship soon thereafter.

On one occasion during my service afloat (as a GS-9), I received a call from Flight ops. *"You have a visitor who has arrived aboard without notice"*. Upon further inquiry, I determined that it was **SA Dave Kerr.** SA Kerr advised that he was visiting me to administer my GS-11 promotional examination. So, with no advance preparation, I completed the required written exam and was advised that I would be recommended for advancement. I am not aware of anyone else who was administered a GS-11 promotional exam while afloat in the Tonkin Gulf. I was subsequently promoted to GS-11.

In October 1972 I was directed to helo immediately to the *USS Kitty Hawk (CV-63)* due to a riot involving multiple racial-driven assaults. Other SA's from the Philippines quickly arrived. Our *game plan* was to attempt to document and investigate each incident of an assault or other violent crime. After many interviews, we were able to identify several assailants who could be linked with a specific victim and assault incident. I recall that SA's **Vern McDonald** and **John Odom** provided valuable guidance and assistance. As the junior SA, I welcomed the presence and leadership of these senior agents."

{Author's note: SA Robbins doesn't specifically mention the deployment schedule, but the first half of this deployment (Sept - Dec 1972) was -in part - as follows

-3-23 Oct: at Yankee Station

-1 -9 Nov: at Yankee Station

-19-31 Dec: at Yankee Station

Yankee Station was, as most know, a fixed location off Vietnam. The same report also contains the following very interesting information regarding the late December Yankee Station ops:]

"ENTERPRISE and CVW 14 took part in stepped up "Linebacker" strikes against North Vietnam. These strikes were flown by Navy all-weather aircraft against the most heavily defended targets of the entire Vietnam War. Railroad facilities, power plants, communication facilities, military airfields, missile equipped patrol craft and vehicle support facilities in both the Hanoi and Haiphong areas were struck during this period. While A6 and A7 attack aircraft were pounding enemy targets, a CVW 14 F4J Phantom flying in support of these strikes downed a North Vietnamese Mig 21 on the out-skirts of Hanoi on 28 December. The subsequent cease-fire throughout Vietnam in January 1973 followed by the release of the first group of US POWs in February resulted not only from long years of negotiations but also in large measure because of the bravery, determination and professional performance of the men of Task Force 77 - performance typified by ENTERPRISE and CVW 14 strike operations during December 1972.

Visitors during this period included the Secretary of the Navy, the Honorable John W. WARNER; Commander-in-Chief, US Pacific Fleet, Admiral Bernard J. CLAREY, USN and Commander SEVENTH Fleet, Vice Admiral J. 0. HOLLOWAY 111, USN, all of whom spent Christmas aboard ENTERPRISE."

Source: https://www.history.navy.mil/content/dam/nhhc/research/archives/command-operation-reports/ship-command-operation-reports/e/enterprise-cvn-65-viii/pdf/1972.pdf

Chapter 9: **Terrorism / Protective Service**

In 1988 the US Government printed a pamphlet titled *Terrorist Group Profiles* in which these groups and their activities were defined and delineated. This pamphlet was published under the signatures of then-President George H. W. Bush and then-Secretary of Defense Frank Carlucci III. Terrorism is defined as "**premeditated, politically motivated violence . . . usually perpetrated to influence an audience**." In regard to Americans as targets, Secretary Carlucci states: "**The United States represents a prime target for terrorist groups because of our commitment to political reform and constructive change. To terrorists reform is anathema, for it represents continuation of the system they abhor and coopts the revolution they hope to lead.**"

Recent foreign terrorism against Americans is primarily linked to Middle Eastern issues. In fact one can debate the definitions of terrorism and war, and where one ends and the other begins. What follows is a sampling drawn from this pamphlet of early terrorist acts directly targeting US Naval and Marine Corps personnel. NCIS SAs likely investigated and / or conducted after-action analysis on these incidents.

Republic of the Philippines: *New People's Army* wanted to replace the government with a Communist regime and erode support of the populace for continued US military presence
-1974 April: Three US Marines were murdered near Subic Bay Naval Base

S/A George McClellan, perimeter guard at NPA ambush site of three senior US Navy SeeBee officers inspecting new road. Subic Bay, RP, 1974

-1987 Oct: Two American servicemen, an American retiree, and a bystander were murdered.

Puerto Rico: *Macheteros* **wanted** to wage a war against US colonial imperialism, and create support for a separate Puerto Rican nation.
-1979 Dec: Bombed a US Navy bus, killing two sailors.

-1982 May: In an ambush outside of a San Juan nightclub killed one sailor and wounded three others. Regarding this bus bombing: 35 years later, in 2014, terrorist Juan Galloza Acevedo was arrested and convicted. Reportedly he played a minor role in the ambush. He was sentenced to five years in prison. **NCIS SA Tim Quick**, when interviewed, said, "he obviously didn't expect to see us . . . we see potential for additional arrests."

Greece: *Revolutionary Organization 17 November* opposed imperialism and capitalism and wanted to force Greece out of NATO and end US military presence in Greece.
-1983 Nov: USN Captain George Tsantes assassinated
-1988 June: USN Captain William "Bill" Nordeen assassinated

El Salvador: *Clara Elizabeth Ramirez Front (CERF)* (parent name *FPL*) wanted to erode public support for the Salvadoran Government and target US personnel who were involved in supporting this government.
-1983 May: Shot and killed LCDR Albert Schaufelberger, as he sat in his auto.

Italy: *Red Brigades* opposed the presence of NATO and wanted to destroy the Government of Italy and imperialist multinational corporations.
-1981 Dec: Kidnapped US Army Brigadier General James Dozier in Verona. He was held for 42 days until freed in a rescue operation by Italian counterterrorist forces. [From article published March 10, 2012. Three decades ago, Dozier was the world's most famous hostage and his captors, the *Red Brigades*, were Europe's most feared and bloody terrorist organization. Dozier, now 80, went back to Italy, perhaps for

the last time, to meet the members of the police special operations unit who liberated him in one of the most daring rescue raids of those dramatic years in Italian history.] *Source: www.reuters.com/news/picture/general-kidnapped-in-1981*

This Dozier kidnapping led to **Operation Red Blanke**t. A Protective Service Operation (bodyguards) put in place following the kidnapping of BGen Dozier, was a w*atershed event* in the history of NCIS. In a first of its kind operation, NCIS sent teams of bodyguards to Italy to provide protective service details. Those protected were flag officers stationed at NATO South command in Naples, one senior civilian at the same command, plus the Commander, Sixth Fleet in Gaeta, Italy. The threat was from terrorists. Many NCIS SAs have memories of this time.

SA Craig Elliott, was assigned to NCIS Naples at the time extensive protective service operations began. He writes that it was *difficult to provide protective service to the area admirals due to small office staffing. We were happy when the other NCIS agents showed up from around the states to take over for us*

SA Tricia Mansell (author) writes: I wasn't with the first wave of NCIS SAs to arrive for this detail, however, I went early on in what I think was the second group. At the time we all stayed for several months, staggering our arrivals and departures so that each detail of four members was turned over one at a time, and not all at once. This lent stability to the teams. The vehicles in use as chase cars were stick shifts; some agents had never driven a stick shift. Driving fast in and around hilly Naples, where people often make their own lanes, and don't pay attention to traffic lights, is a brutal way to learn to drive a stick shift. Fortunately for me, I had owned such a vehicle in college.

Work days were long, as we provided protection from the time the Admiral left his home until he returned home for the night. (Senior officers often had evening functions to attend.) Once in bed, local police watched the home until NCIS agents arrived again early morning. The Admirals each had an assigned car and military driver. Teams were on their own to split up functions, but generally one SA rode with the Admiral in his car, and two more followed in a *chase car*. The fourth agent in the detail either had the day off or had duty in the command center, monitoring radio traffic and actions of all teams in Naples. The duty was challenging, but one good thing is that we worked closely with the Italian *Polizia* and the *Carabiniere*. The latter is a hybrid police / military force and the *law of the land* in Italy.

TWA Airliner: *Hizballah (Islamic Jihad)* wanted to establish a Shi'a Islamic state in Lebanon, eliminate non-Islamic influences, and force Western interests out of the region.

-1985 June: *Hizballah* hijacked TWA flight 847, originating in Cairo and bound for the US, with several stops en route. The hijacking occurred upon leaving Athens. Of note is their intentional murder of passenger Robert Stethem, a USN diver. Also, 39 US citizens were held hostage for 17 days in Beirut.

3 Terror Attacks That Changed NCIS and the Nation

1) October 23, 1983, **US Marine Barracks bombing**: Over 240 military personnel were killed when a suicide bomber, driving a large truck filled with explosives, penetrated the barracks area in Beirut, Lebanon. **Shiite Muslims** claimed responsibility. Many of the marines killed were members of Camp Lejuene's 24th Marine Amphibious Unit. In a remembrance celebration 30 years later (2013) USMC

Commandant General James Amos said, "this bombing signaled the start of a new kind of war. . . We never forgive nor will we ever forget." *(source: cbsnews.com/top-marine-survivors)*

2) October 12, 2000 **USS Cole (DDG-67) bombing**: 17 USN sailors were killed and 39 were injured in a blast aboard ship. This ship was docked in Aden harbor (Yemen) for a routine fuel stop. Mooring was completed at 0930, refueling started at 1030, and around 1118 local time a small craft approached the ship at which time explosives were planted against the hull of the ship. The explosion caused a 40 X 60 foot gash in the ship's port side. **Osama bin Laden / al-Qaeda** claimed responsibility. . . A 2010 article written in the Navy Times discusses the bombing of the USS Cole ten years earlier, specifically quoting Captain Sam McCormick, the anti-terrorism protection officer for Fleet Forces Command. He said this bombing was a watershed event for the Navy, causing a huge amount of change. "Doctrine, organization, material, logistics, facilities and personnel requirements have been modified and training has been totally revamped," he said. "Ships in port employ protective zones, security barriers and harbor security patrols; high value units are escorted in and out of Port." He also said ""One of the biggest pieces that came out of the attack on the Cole was truly a mindset change in the Navy, When you have a successful attack in which, tragically, 17 sailors were killed and a billion-dollar warship was significantly damaged, that changes the psyche of the Navy." Source: archive NavyTimes.com

3) September 11, 2001 **World Trade Center (WTC) and Pentagon bombings**: Hijacked commercial jetliners crashed into the twin towers of the WTC in New York City and the Pentagon in Washington, DC. One jetliner was downed by passengers in a field in rural Pennsylvania. **Islamic al-Qaeda** deemed responsible. Often referred to as 9/11, the attacks resulted in extensive death and destruction, triggering major US initiatives to combat terrorism. Over 3,000 people (including more than 400 police officers and firefighters) were killed. **Specifically at the Pentagon:** At 9:37 am hijackers aboard Flight 77 crashed the plane into the western façade of the Pentagon in Washington, D.C., killing 59 aboard the plane and 125 military and civilian personnel inside the building. Source: *http://www.history.com/topics/9-11-attacks*

Aftermath of these 3 attacks

The aftermath of the **Marine Barracks bombing** is discussed in the Special Agent Afloat section that also discussed NCIS office Beirut.

SA Cathy Clements was interviewed and recalled her work following the **bombing of the USS Cole**. Assigned to the European Field Office, Major Case Response Team, she was called to assist. She, along with fellow **SA Donival Thomson** boarded a Lear Jet bound for Aden, Yemen. Upon arrival they were briefed by SAs who had come from the NCIS office in Bahrain and were already in Yemen: **Mike Dorsey, Mike Marks, Larry Mullins, Harry Richardson**, and Physical Security Specialist **Gary Chamberlin**.

SA Clements' immediate observations were that the ship was dirty with diesel fuel, still afloat but listing, and the crew was very somber. The ship's Commanding Officer briefed the NCIS agents and gave them a tour of the ship and spaces to work in. She helped extricate bodies from the ship and then assisted in the post-blast investigation. Along with other agents, SA Clements swept the ship to collect evidence; they collected only foreign materials.

For weeks after the **9/11 attack of the Pentagon,** NCIS agents - with a large team of others - conducted the crime scene investigation. Those involved surely worked with sadness, but gave their all to work under unimaginable circumstances. The investigation included extrication of bodies and collecting evidence.

The aftermath included the realization that a counterterrorism command center would need to become a task force, eventually morphing into a Counterterrorism Division. The Antiterrorism Alert Center (ATAC) would become the Multiple Threat Alert Center (MTAC).

These events are recounted in an article written by Petty Officer Barbara Shupe, USNR titled <u>Operation Noble Eagle: D. C.'s Largest Crime Scene.</u> Below are selections of memories written and displayed in this article:

"When we left the interstate and saw the Pentagon, it was even worse than we thought. We'd seen it on TV, but actually looking at it, there was no comparison . " **SA Dan Rice**

I Remember reaching through the ashes to find things. The soot and rubble were burning hot, so that you'd have to step back and make sure your rubber boots weren't melting." **SA Dan Rice**

photo by D. Parlato

In a makeshift command center at NCIS HQ, the Secretary of the Navy, the Chief of Naval Operations, and their staffs get the latest information on the damage to the Pentagon and efforts to account for the missing.

"When SA (Mike) McLean played "Amazing Grace" on his pipes it was so moving. A lot of people walked away with tears in their eyes."
Marine Corps Gunny Sgt. Mary Odrick

More Protective Service Details (PSDs)

It is not immediately certain when the first ONI / NCIS PSD occurred, but **SA Ted Miller** produced a Memorandum of Appreciation from Supervising Agent **Sherm Bliss** to a dozen NCIS agents involved in the May 14 and 15, 1971 PSD for the Secretary of the Navy (SECNAV) and Chief of Naval Operations (CNO). Those SAs recognized for working this detail were: **SAs Brooks, Fitzpatrick, Focht, Grim, Hansen, Jesse, Koslowski, Miller, Reis, Sundstrom, Turner, and Wall.**

An article published by NCIS in 1975 briefly acquaints SAs with PSD protocols and states formalized training will be in the near future. In addition to responding to occasional requests for assistance from the US Secret Service, C is specifically tasked to protect SECNAV, CNO, and other high-ranking military officials. According to this article, the three primary reasons for protective service are to prevent assassination, to prevent assault, or to prevent embarrassment. The two secondary reasons are to prevent kidnapping and to maintain a schedule.

In the event of an attack SAs in the (inner) detail *must resist the need to go after the attacker and instead stay in a protective mode.* To this end, the four considerations are: 1) Arms reach, which means the SA must not vacate his position if the attacker is within arm's reach of the protectee 2) Sound off (as in 'gun left') 3) Cover the protectee 4) Evacuate the protectee.

+ + + + + +

SA Ed Jex wrote a comprehensive article about the first Protective Service Operation (PSO) sent into Iraq in June 2003. He led the team of eight agents; four of which went immediately upon notice and four others joined in two weeks. He was among the first four, and the following are excerpts covering a period from July through October 2003 on this PSO. Beside SA Jex, the other team members were **SAs Mike Adams**, **Joe Brummond**, **Pat Byrne**, **Rich Campbell**, **Yale Carnevale**, **Greg Huska**, and **Ricky Rendon**.

He advised the first four agents received no special training, they crossed the border from Kuwait to Iraq driving in two un-armored vehicles, and spent the first night in the Baghdad Sheraton Hotel which had no electricity. They sat on the balcony and watched tracer fire and explosions throughout the city. The next day they drove 60 miles to Al Hillah, which would be their operating base. With no established protocols they scrounged for weapons and equipment, established an office, and set the protocols that would subsequently be used to train agents for PSOs.

SA Jex details specific incidents by date; a sampling summary is presented here. They conducted many emergency evacuations of their principles while under small arms fire; rammed vehicles attempting to penetrate their motorcade; thwarted an attack in Ramadi; narrowly missed an IED attack in Fallujah; drove through an ambush that killed one soldier; were fired upon in their compound and in their motorcade. Of note is they took their principle to clandestine meetings in the Shiite areas of Najaf; areas considered too dangerous for Coalition Forces to enter. Four days after one of these meetings the leader their principle had met was killed in a massive car bombing at the same location. They took a principle to a building in Hillah; the same building was blown up the next day.

SA Jex added, "We were there from June through November, during the hottest months of the year. We used open, unarmored vehicles and stood post in the elements. We were often under fire, and routinely worked without support from Coalition military forces. Usually, we were on our own. We worked for 139 straight days, with no time off. Fifteen to twenty hour days were standard.

On the more fun side of things, we were in the ruins of ancient Babylon numerous times. We climbed the Tower of Babel. We were at the tomb of the Prophet Ezekiel. It was perhaps the most intense experience of my career thus far."

SA Paul Sparks writes about *OPERATION FIREBALL*, a PSO designed to protect USMC LtCol Oliver North from threats. According to SA Sparks, threats came from those who did not approve of his actions pertaining to the Iran-Contra Affair. Threats also came from Colonel Muammar Qaddafi, who held LtCol North responsible for air strikes conducted against his home in retaliation for Libyan involvement with terrorism.

In late 1987 SA Sparks was called into the office of **SA Bill Worochock**, the Assistant Director of Counterintelligence at NCIS Headquarters, and informed of the need to protect LtCol North. The PSO was quickly assembled and designed with three shifts of agents, led by shift leaders **SAs Wayne Clookie**, **Kenny Rogers**, and **J.R. Mathis**. The SA team members came from *Mount Up Teams* over all geographic NCIS regions. These teams were SAs who had special training and designation in protective services and had been strategically scattered in different areas. All together over 100 agents were assigned on a rotational basis for a 24/7 PSO of LtCol North for ten months.

On a personal note SA Sparks says LtCol North was a memorable protectee and "there is no doubt that the vast majority of agents on this detail would have followed him into battle." SA Sparks also added, "A Winnebago RV was parked on his home property to use as a command post. Mrs. North made certain it was always well stocked with baked goods and sandwiches."

Photo of LtCol North and SA Paul Sparks

Some history is best displayed in context with events of the same time frame. This chapter captures such history, and is written here in a series captioned

"A Moment in Time"

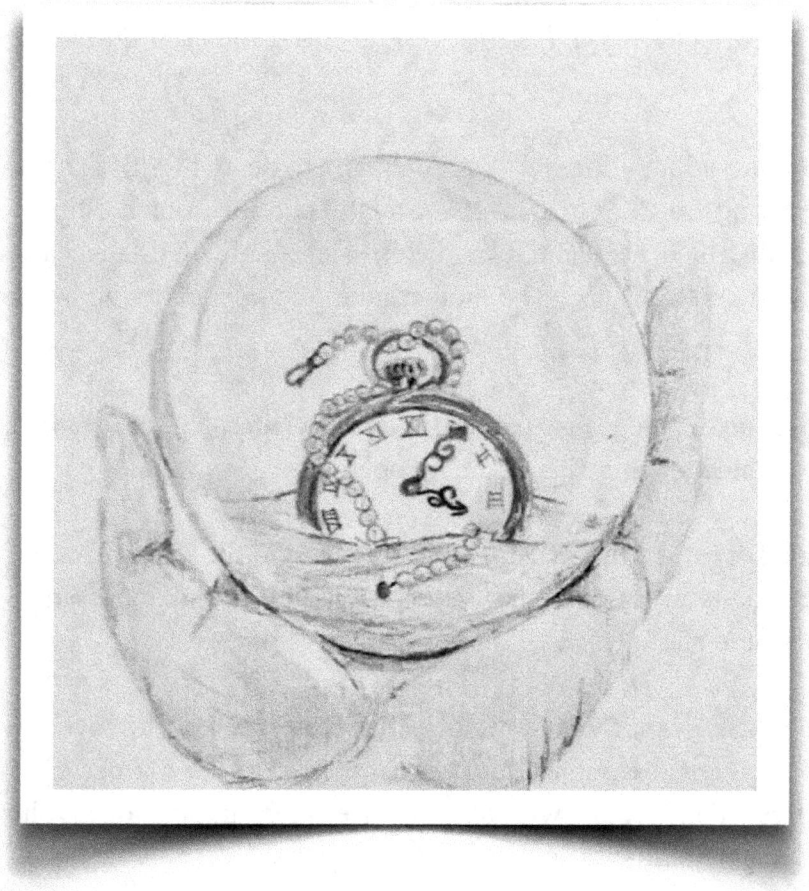

A Moment in Time: Select NCIS Activities Post 9/11

[*Author's Note: NCIS mission activities in the immediate months following 9/11 include some that are typical and ongoing, and others that are directly related to the 9/11 terrorist attack. A sampling of these follows:*]

-**NCIS solved a cold case:** Even though the death of a five month old baby living on the Great Lakes Naval Training Center, Illinois was originally ruled accidental, at the insistence of NCIS the case was reviewed and reopened. The mother admitted to smothering her son to death and was arrested for murder.

-**A high level delegation from Singapore visited NCISHQ** to discuss Force Protection and anti-terrorism operations.

-**NCIS Director Dave Brant flew to the Middle East**, meeting with NCIS agents in Bahrain and Dubai, as well as with Ambassadors and law enforcement personnel throughout the region.

-**NCIS Mayport, Florida field office concluded a murder case.** A USN Lieutenant Commander was charged with the murder of one of his five month old twin sons. He pled guilty to involuntary manslaughter and was sentenced to nine years.

-NCIS Office in London co-hosted a holiday party at the American Embassy with 300 guests, including law enforcement representatives from several European countries.

-Post 9/11 NCIS has conducted fourteen successful Protective Service Details within New York City.

-NCIS European Field Office recently briefed senior security and law enforcement officials from Slovenia.

-NCIS Northwest Field Office participated in a large operation in and around Seattle, Washington. 200 law enforcement personnel from NCIS, DEA, and local police departments arrested 40 suspects and seized large amounts of drugs, cash, and firearms.

-Seven SAs have been assigned to the War Crimes Tribunal Task Force in Guantanamo Bay, Cuba with others to be assigned shortly.

-NCIS Office in Rota, Spain hosted a conference on security for the Strait of Gibraltar; participants included high level US officials and others from Morocco, Spain, Gibraltar, and England.

-NCIS Director Brant presented an American flag to the Commissioner of the New York City Police Department. The flag had been flown at Iwo Jima by NCIS agents from NCIS office in Okinawa to honor the NYPD officers who had lost their lives in the 9/11 attacks.

-NCIS provided protective service to the "Navy's All-Flag Officers Conference" in Orlando, Florida. They were assisted with this protection by local police. In attendance were 315 Navy Admirals and 50 Senior Executive Service (SES) Officials.

A Moment in Time: 1987 Special Agents Afloat

SPECIAL AGENTS AFLOAT AS OF 1 SEP 87

Ship	Agent(s)
USS LEXINGTON (AVT-16)	Jewel Seawood
USS MIDWAY (CV-41)	Larry Worthington
USS CORAL SEA (CV-43)	Bob Mulligan Tony Albalar
USS FORRESTAL (CV-59)	Paul Martin
USS SARATOGA (CV-60)	Chris Calimer Tim Carruth
USS RANGER (CV-61)	Leon Carroll Mike Donnelly
USS INDEPENDENCE (CV-62)	Steve Smith
USS CONSTELLATION (CV-64)	Des Wieland Jim Lofstrom
USS ENTERPRISE (CVN-65)	Mark Giordano Leo Miller
USS AMERICA (CV-66)	Dan Rice
USS JOHN F. KENNEDY (CV-67)	Steve Gorden Scott James
USS NIMITZ (CVN-68)	Mitch Anderson
USS DWIGHT T. EISENHOWER (CVN-69)	Rich Osborne
USS CARL VINSON (CVN-70)	Guy Molina Rick Jordan
USS THEODORE ROOSEVELT (CVN-71)	Steve Simpson Don McBride
USS MISSOURI (BB-63)	Bob McCutchin

As shown on the list, **SA Steve Gorden** was on the *USS John F. Kennedy* (CV-67) as the senior SAA. True, but as an example of what can happen on deployment, he did not complete that assignment. An agent on the *USS Dwight D. Eisenhower* (CVN-69) departed unexpectedly. **SA Gorden** was then transferred to that warship for a six-month deployment, again, as Senior SAA.

That explains why the photo of him below is on the deck of the *Eisenhower* while in port Sicily early 1988. The other photo is of his stateroom on the *Eisenhower*.

SA Gorden remembers harrowing experiences such as being winched from a helo to the deck of one or another small warships tossing about in rough seas, and working a death investigation in the hold of an ammunition ship surrounded by bombs and other munitions. Some of the better times were doing threat assessments and launching off the deck of the carrier. But, like most SAAs, his greater memories are positive. As he says, "Unless you have been an agent afloat you can never understand the depth of the experience, the true challenges, and the feelings of accomplishments."

A Moment in Time: Plank Owners in 1987

NCIS periodically publishes a **Plank Owners' List** which lists the active agents by seniority. The below list was published in 1987. During this time the plank holders were hired between 1959 and 1964.

NIS Plank Owners' List

In keeping with time-honored traditions, the Naval Investigative Service periodically publishes the "Plank Owners List" showing the top 25 Special Agents in terms of service. The "Plank Owners" as of 1 October 1987 are listed below:

	NAME	DUSTA	NIS DATE
1.	Kuehl, Winston	11HQ	23 AUG 59
2.	King, Laurence P.	03GL	09 NOV 59
3.	Naylor, Joseph F.	0026	16 MAR 61
4.	Barrows, Robert J.	80HN	13 JUL 61
5.	Brannon, Thomas E.	60HQ	05 MAR 62
6.	Butler, Lawrence W.	03BN	01 JUN 62
7.	Black, Verner Gene	06MP	27 AUG 62
8.	Jett, Charles D.	12AL	28 AUG 62
9.	McKee, J. Brian	0002	01 SEP 62
10.	Reilly, Peter	000Y	02 SEP 62
11.	Tatum, Allan D.	81HQ	24 SEP 62
12.	Carl, John W., Jr.	12WH	10 OCT 62
13.	Skinner, Larry V.	11LB	15 OCT 62
14.	Seehorn, Frederick R.	0024	07 JAN 63
15.	McCullah, Lanny E.	0022	15 APR 63
16.	Perrin, Anthony W.	11PE	20 MAY 63
17.	Olson, John V.	12MA	27 MAY 63
18.	Williams, Thomas C.	0026	03 JUN 63
19.	Usrey, Dennis E.	05HQ	17 JUN 63
20.	Stovall, Harry J.	11ET	29 JUL 63
21.	McBride, Daniel A.	83SU	09 SEP 63
22.	Musante, Paul V.	06RL	01 OCT 63
23.	McDonald, Vincent K.	11NC	18 OCT 63
24.	Childs, Richard E.	0028	18 NOV 63
25.	Brandt, Joseph W.	06CS	04 JAN 64

A Moment in Time: 1980s Espionage

Elsewhere in this book is a chapter about the 1980s being considered the *Decade of the Spy,* and discussing several highly visible spy cases and operations.

In addition to those cases addressed elsewhere, the following were subjects of 1980s espionage investigations:

>Stephen A. Baba 1981
>Michael R. Murphy 1981
>Brian E. Slavens 1982
>Robert W. Ellis 1983
>Jeffery L. Pickering 1983
>Hans P. Wold 1983
>Robert E. Cordrey 1984
>Samuel L. Morison 1984
>Francis X. Pizzo 1984
>Michael T. Tobias 1984
>Jay C. Wolf 1984
>Stephen D. Hawkins 1985
>Robert D. Haguewood 1986
>Craig D. Kunkle 1989
>Randall S. Bush 1989
>Michael H Allen 1986

A Moment in Time: Homicides Camp Lejeune 1980/81

NCIS **SA D. A. Cobb** analyzed five homicide investigations at Camp Lejeune, North Carolina occurring between July 1980 and April 1981. What follows is a short description of these cases (dispositions are as of 1981):

#1: July 1980 In an effort to avoid paying a narcotics related debt, subject and co-subject killed victim. They put the body in the trunk of a car borrowed from a third party friend. This friend found the body, which led to the investigation. Subject sentenced to death and co-subject to 40 years.

#2: November 1980 Victim, a known local prostitute, was shot and killed and her body was discovered in a mattress cover located in a wooded area adjoining base housing. Suspects were developed but there is lack of evidence sufficient to prosecute at this time.

#3: December 1980 Subject, who allegedly participated in homosexual pornographic videos, was paranoid over previous advances of victims. Fearing he would be sodomized by them he shot and killed them. Subject is presently confined in the psychiatric ward of a veteran's hospital.

#4: February 1981 Subject lured victim to an isolated area on base purportedly to sell victim drugs. Subject and co-subject killed victim with a shotgun. Investigation revealed they were leaders of a robbery ring operating aboard base. Subject received death penalty and co-subject received 50 years.

#5: April 1981 In a wooded area near the base enlisted club, subject and co-subject smoked marijuana with victim and then demanded money in a robbery attempt. Victim declined, subjects

both pulled handguns and killed victim with one shot to the area of the eye. Subject sentenced to life and co-subject to 40 years.

Homicide Analysis by SA Cobb:

Factors:

-All 5 cases involved drugs

-Subjects of all 5 cases had prior disciplinary problems

-Premeditation was prevalent

-Robbery as a motive was present in two cases

Successful resolution occurred with:

-Sufficient agents to assist in investigation

- Close cooperation with pathologists and medical professionals

- Thorough crime scene examination

- Positive benefit derived from working with the trial counsel at the earliest possible moment in the case.

A Moment in Time: October 1971 *USS Constellation* Prepares to Deploy to Vietnam

In October 1971 the *USS Constellation (CV 64)* deployed to Southeast Asia. According to the local media most crew members ignored protests by the group *Nonviolent Action* who had spent $27,000 in a "stop the Constellation from deploying" campaign.

Nine crew members, however, sought refuge at a local area Roman Catholic Church. In a flurry of legal activity ultimately the Navy prevailed. Warrants were issued for the arrest of these nine sailors.

Media reports "when church officials argued that arrest would violate the moral sanctity of the church, government officials advised that the US had no formal agreement with the Vatican providing for the use of Catholic churches as sanctuaries".

These nine sailors surrendered peacefully to 20 NCIS SAs and US Marshals at the church. These sailors were then placed in a brig at North Island Naval Air Station and shortly thereafter flown aboard a C2 military aircraft out to the *USS Constellation*.

In order to counter threats and unrest, **SA Ted Miller** and **SA Pete Reilly** sailed aboard this warship for about a week.

In a similar case, nine crew members of the *USS Kitty Hawk (CV 63)* sought sanctuary in local churches just a few months later in February 1972. President Nixon had ordered this ship to deploy a month early in order to reinforce naval strength off the coast of Vietnam. **SA Ted Miller** remembers that he assisted in escorting these sailors, via helicopter, to board the ship about 25 miles off shore.

USS Constellation (CV-64)

USS Kitty Hawk (CV-63)

A Moment in Time: 2015
Sampling of NCIS Sexual-Related Cases/Prosecutions early 2015

-On March 5 US Navy Electronics Technician 3rd Class Rashad Long received a 19-year prison sentence after pleading guilty to one count of attempted sexual assault and five counts of sexual assault.

-On March 19 Terrance Brown received an eight-year prison sentence and three years of Federal probation after pleading guilty in Federal court to the sexual abuse of a minor. He will also have to register as a sex offender. NCIS initiated an investigation after the victim's mother reported that Brown was caught sexually assaulting her child behind a house aboard Naval Support Activity Mid-South in Millington, Tenn.

-On March 24 USMC Private First Class Dee Harris (male) was sentenced to 6-20 years in prison after being found guilty in a Michigan court of criminal sexual misconduct in the first degree.

-On March 31 USMC Staff Sergeant James Allen Hale received a 26-year prison sentence after being found guilty of rape and kidnapping.

-On April 2 USMC Gunnery Sergeant Ike Chisolm received a 30-year prison sentence after being found guilty of seven counts of aggravated sexual contact with a child and six counts of sexual abuse of a child.

-On April 3 NCIS assisted Rhode Island State Police (RISP) and Homeland Security Investigations in the arrest of Adam Cobb, a research professor at the US Naval War College and Director of the Mahan Advanced Research Project, for allegedly possessing and distributing child pornography. The investigation began in January, when the National Center for Missing and Exploited Children reported to the RISP Internet Crimes Against Children Unit that someone from Rhode Island had uploaded child pornography on Tumblr, a blogging site. Detectives traced the Internet connection to Cobb's home address and, on March 5, seized a storage device and computer from his home. They also seized Cobb's government computer and conducted surveillance of him at work and in his vehicle. A forensic review of the devices revealed multiple sexually explicit photos and videos of two minor females, some of which Cobb allegedly sent to a friend. Cobb is being held without bond.

-On April 24 US Navy Lieutenant Jonathan Jones received a 21-year prison sentence after pleading guilty to 1 count of rape, 1 count of sexual assault, and 1 count of taking indecent liberties with a child. He will serve five years pursuant to a pretrial agreement.

-On May 13 US Navy Chief Petty Officer Matthew Beltran was sentenced to five years confinement after being found guilty of attempted rape of a child in the third degree, commercial sex abuse of a minor, and communicating with a minor for immoral purposes.

-On June 9 Desiree Bolyard, wife of a US Marine Corps Master Sergeant, was sentenced to 5 years in prison and 10 years of supervised release after pleading guilty to traveling with the intent to engage in illegal sexual conduct with a minor.

-On June 23 US Navy Petty Officer 1st Class Jeffrey Quichocho was sentenced to four years confinement after being found guilty of one charge of sexual assault and two charges of assault.

-On June 26 US Navy Seaman Apprentice Hyunho Yoon was sentenced to six months confinement after pleading guilty to sexual assault.

A Moment in Time: 2015
Sampling of NCIS Foreign Relations Matters early 2015

February: NCIS teamed with the US Coast Guard to provide vessel boarding training to Ghanaian maritime security agencies, including the Ghana Marine Police Unit, the Ghana Navy, and Ghana Fisheries Enforcement Unit. The participating Ghanaian agencies are planning to form a joint Ghanaian boarding team as a result of the course.

March: NCIS Force Protection Detachment (FPD) Ghana, the Europe and Africa Field Office, and the Security Training Assistance and Assessment Teams (STAAT) Atlantic conducted the first STAAT Atlantic Interoperability Program for 32 local law enforcement and security personnel in Togo. FPD Ghana coordinated the seminar in response to US Africa Command's efforts to combat illicit trafficking through the FPD's area of responsibility.

March: NCIS conducted a subject matter expert exchange on countering illicit maritime trafficking with 227 South African law enforcement officers during seminars in Cape Town and Durban, including briefings on drug trafficking trends and trafficking routes in the Middle East and South Africa region.

April: Representatives from SEFO, the NCISHQ Biometrics Branch, and Homeland Security Investigations conducted capacity building in Cartagena with the Colombian Navy. Colombian sailors were taught how to use biometric technology to combat terrorism, transnational crime, narcotics trafficking, and human smuggling, and how to use the handheld biometric equipment

April: **Director Andrew Traver**, Senior Intelligence Officer **Ricardo Karakadze**, and Southeast Field Office (SEFO) Supervisor **Andrew Snowdon** met with US embassy, US and Colombian law enforcement, and Colombian naval leaders in Bogota and Cartagena to assess current and future NCIS support to the Combating Transnational Organized Crime (CTOC) and force protection missions.

April: Special Agents briefed four members of a French naval ship's boarding team on proper boarding techniques and procedures in preparation of the French Navy assuming command of Combined Task Force 150 (CTF-150) the following day. Briefs focused on maritime law enforcement support to counter-narcotics operations, boarding techniques and procedures, narcotics collection and documentation, and tactical questioning.

May: NCIS agents from Norfolk, Va., conducted consecutive interoperability program seminars on detection of installation surveillance and protective service operations for law enforcement officers in Willemstad, Curacao. Attendees included officers of the Curacao Police Force's VIP Protection Division, Volunteer Corps of Curacao, and the Royal Dutch Military Police.

May: NCIS agents conducted capacity-building seminars on port security and maritime interdiction operations for Cameroon port security officials aboard the Douala Naval Base. The seminars were funded by Africa Partnership Station, US Naval Forces Africa's flagship maritime security cooperation program.

June: Principal Computer Scientist **Ed So** spoke about the NCIS Cyber Division and network intrusion response to assembled Australian State and Federal law enforcement officers during cybercrime workshops in Australia.

A Moment in Time: 2015

Sampling of **NCIS related investigations/prosecutions in early 2015**

June: Khairullozhon Matanov was sentenced to 30 months in prison and 3 years of supervised release for obstructing the investigation of the 2013 Boston Marathon bombings. In March Matanov pleaded guilty to one count of falsifying, concealing, and covering up a material fact in a Federal investigation and one count of making materially false statements in a Federal investigation. According to an investigation by the FBI's Joint Terrorism Task Force, *of which an NCIS Special Agent serves as a principal case agent*, Matanov took steps to conceal the extent of his friendship, contact, and communication with the bombers, Dzhokhar and Tamerlan, as well as any information and views he held related to terrorism and the Tsarnaevs.

March: Special Agents from the NCIS Singapore office deployed to Mumbai to assist INTERPOL in the debriefing of 39 Indian nationals who had been held captive by Somali pirates for several years until their recent release. Deploying at the request of the INTERPOL Maritime Piracy Task Force and in coordination with the Government of India, NCIS interviewed each former hostage using a translator to gather intelligence on key Somali piracy networks. During the interviews, the former hostages detailed their experiences in captivity, identified several piracy leaders, and provided other valuable intelligence.

May: Special Agents from NCIS Dubai and the Middle East conducted interviews of several crew members who served aboard the Marshall Islands-flagged M/V Maersk Tigris when it was detained by the Government of Iran and held illegally outside the port of Bandar Abbas for more than a week beginning April 28. Iran claimed it seized the container ship because of a commercial dispute with Denmark's Maersk group, which chartered the vessel, causing concern for the security of shipping lanes in the strategic strait and prompting the United States to send vessels to monitor the situation. The interviews, which took place in Dubai's Port Jebel Ali and yielded critical intelligence, were coordinated by NCIS with support from INTERPOL, the FBI, UAE State security, and the United Kingdom Marine Trade Operations. NCIS also collected fingerprints and other biometrics from the vessel.

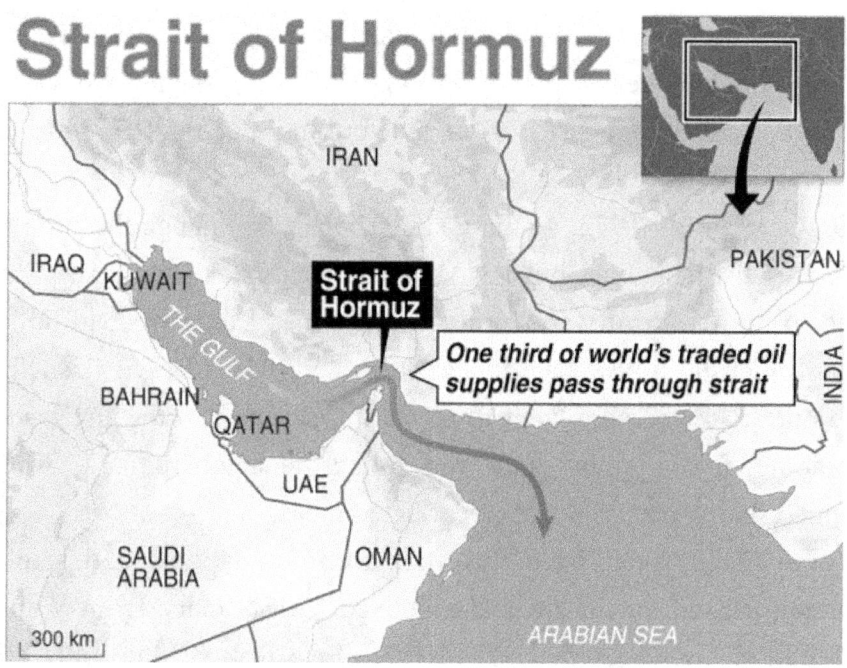

A Moment in Time: October 29, 1972

*[Author's note: **SA Catherine (Schanz) Clements** is married to **SA Lee Clements**. Her siblings include Marie, a graduate of the US Naval Academy, and Dorothy who retired as a Lt Col from the US Air Force. Her father, **SA Harry Jerome Schanz**, graduated from high school, spent four years in the US Coast Guard, and then attended college before becoming an NCIS agent in 1963. He served in Milwaukee, Wisconsin and Yokosuka, Japan, and from Japan was sent for temporary duty aboard the USS Saratoga (CV-60).]*

An article written by **SA William Blow** describes the death of **SA Harry Schanz** as a result of a fire aboard the ship in 1972. SA Schanz was not a Special Agent Afloat on the ship, but rather he was there at the request of the ship's Commanding Officer for an agent to come aboard to pursue new leads in a narcotics investigation. The request was sent on October 7, 1972, and SA Schanz, assigned to NCIS Yokosuka, arrived onboard for an indeterminate amount of time on October 15, 1972.

On October 29, 1972, a young sailor began to change the filter in the Navy Distillate Fuel Oil #2 Alpha boiler duplex strainer . . . he stayed to make sure it was draining properly and then went to boiler repair to pick up a new bag and gasket . . . a Class Bravo flash fire broke out . . . the ship went to General Quarters . . . the fire lasted only about five minutes and was fought tenaciously . . . when contained search parties went into affected areas.

Three people died from this fire, all from hypoxia and smoke inhalation caused by the fire: The body of IMSN Gary Lynn Weller was found in a passageway and the body of AA Robert Michael Norris was discovered a short distance away inside a doorway. The body of **NCIS SA Harry Schanz** was discovered in a shower / bathroom area located a short distance from Shanz's stateroom. Notably, subsequent formal investigation determined the nearest intercom speaker was 40 to 50 feet away, thus the General Quarters announcement would have been barely audible and not at all discernible.

A memorial service was held aboard the USS Saratoga on November 4, 1972. SA Schanz's body was transported to Yokosuka for a memorial service, and then flown to Chicago, Illinois for burial.

A Moment in Time: The Ties that Bind

NCIS SA Tom Boley was hired as an agent in 1974 and retired in 1999, after 25 years of service. Prior to his job with NCIS, Tom was on active duty as a US Army communications specialist; he was fluent in both writing and speaking Japanese. Tom was raised in Kansas, and he married a childhood girlfriend, Judy. Together they had one child, a son named Brett.

Tom had tremendous talents to offer NCIS, not the least of which was that he became a certified aircraft pilot. NCIS today has an aviation - surveillance program. The *roots* of this program were started in 1987 by SA Tom Boley.

Tom's father flew P-40s during WW II in China, Burma, and India, and he later flew a small private plane in connection with his business. Tom grew up loving flying, with dreams of one day becoming a pilot. He accomplished that; thus cementing ties with his father in aviation.

Tom's son, **Brett Boley**, grew up to become an NCIS Special Agent. Tom has said: "It is hugely gratifying to see children grow up and spread their wings, but there was something extra in the bond when my son Brett followed me into NCIS law enforcement."

Another generation of ties that bind.

A Moment in Time: 2001

SA John Harris (right) retired after 29 years of NCIS service, and was presented with his shadowbox by the Director.

SA Harris served many overseas tours, accompanied by his wife Barb, who took the opportunity to teach in DoD schools. Their son, Greg, and daughter, Lucy, both became NCIS agents.

A Moment in Time: February 1982

SA Tricia Mansell (author) writes: In late February, two weeks after I had surgery to have my tonsils removed, and 2 weeks before my 30th birthday, I found myself in the Sheraton airport hotel in Philadelphia, Pennsylvania. The plan was to stay the night and leave the next day for *Operation Red Blanket* bodyguard duty in Italy.

For the first time I met my travel mates; one was **SA Joan Barron**. We arrived in Italy to find we were assigned to separate teams, but we were scheduled to be roommates in the hotel in Naples.

The first morning in Italy I laughed when Joan blew the electricity by plugging in her hair dryer, plugging in an iron, and turning on too many lights - all at once! She called for assistance, telling the front desk she had wet hair and needed this fixed, and then opened the door shortly to find, not a maintenance person, but a bellman with a handful of towels. Joan and I became great friends, never stopped laughing, and kept in touch for the remainder of our lives.

Through the years Joan's assignments included Okinawa, Japan, Bahrain, San Diego, New London, and Washington DC.

Joan wrote to my daughter's 6th grade class while she was in Bahrain, and they wrote back. This running dialog, for a whole year, taught the students so much about the world. And, it included frequent stories of her Dalmatian dog, *Boqua*, which is Arabic for *Spot*. She told the kids *Boqua* mostly behaves, but *"sometimes Boqua pretends she only understands Arabic!"*

Like many other NCIS employees have experienced, one moment in time can make for a lifetime friendship.

A Delightful Way to Close this NCIS History Book *is with*

CARICATURES

Drawn by
Special Agent *Michael Nagle*
during his service with the
NCIS: 1966 - 1978

SA Nagle was both a talented special agent and a talented caricature artist. His drawings delighted many agents through the years. Following his time with NCIS he became a highly successful attorney, practicing in Southern California, though always staying close to his NCIS roots. And, always remembering his ancestral roots. His father was a Navy fighter pilot killed during WWII in the *Battle of Guadalcanal*.

To all contributors to this sampling of NCIS history

Thanks for the memories!

"SANTA COMES TO VIETNAM" NISO VIETNAM DECEMBER 1967

SPECIAL AGENT BOB BAGSHAW 1967

SPECIAL AGENT GRAHAM BELL 1969

SPECIAL AGENT WALT CLEVELAND 1971

SPECIAL AGENT WALT FOCHT 1975

SPECIAL AGENT DON HERSHBERGER 1976

SPECIAL AGENT WES HOWE 1975

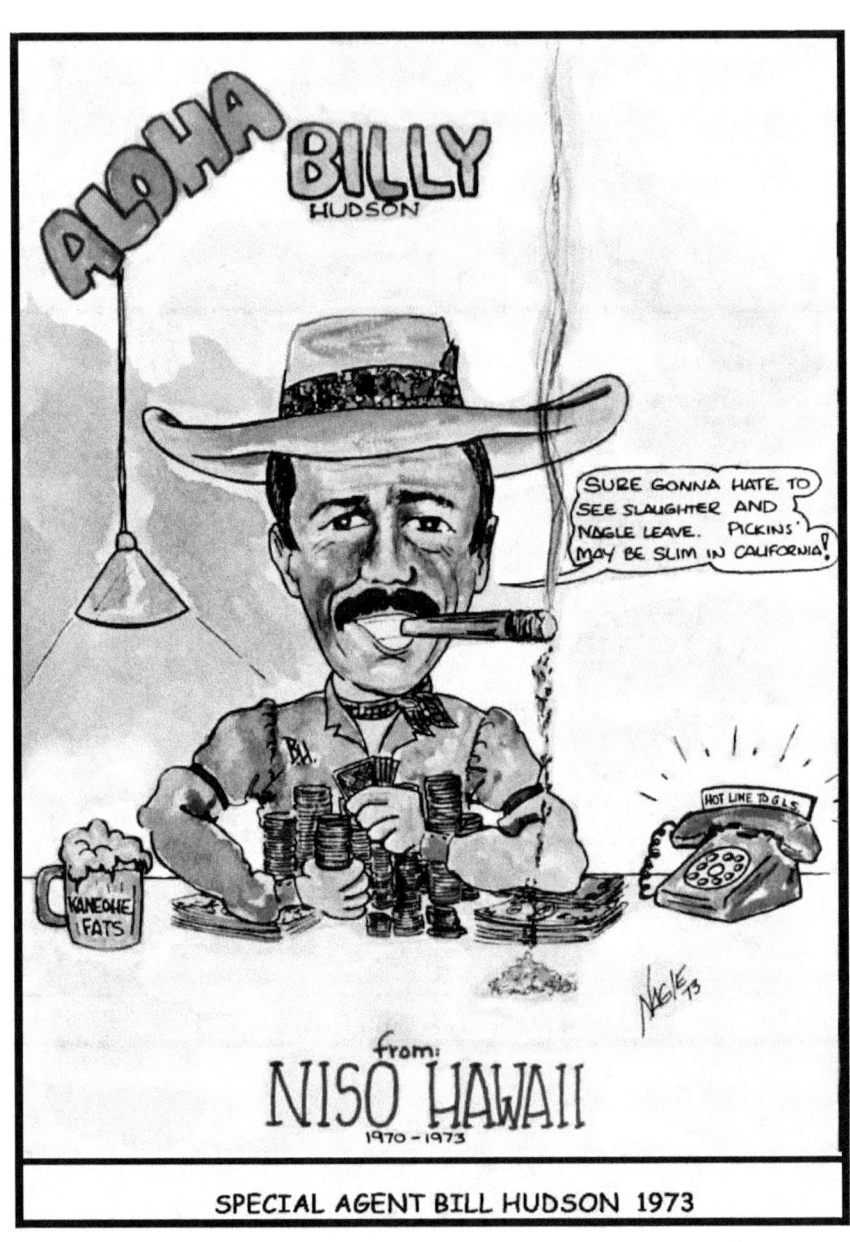

SPECIAL AGENT BILL HUDSON 1973

CDR ROBERT KANE USNR C.O. NISO HAWAII
AND LCDR LYNN SHAFTOE USNR XO NISO HAWAII

SPECIAL AGENT TOM LOUTEN GOES TO P.I. 1966

SPECIAL AGENT KEN NICKEL 1976

SPECIAL AGENT KENT MONTGOMERY 1975

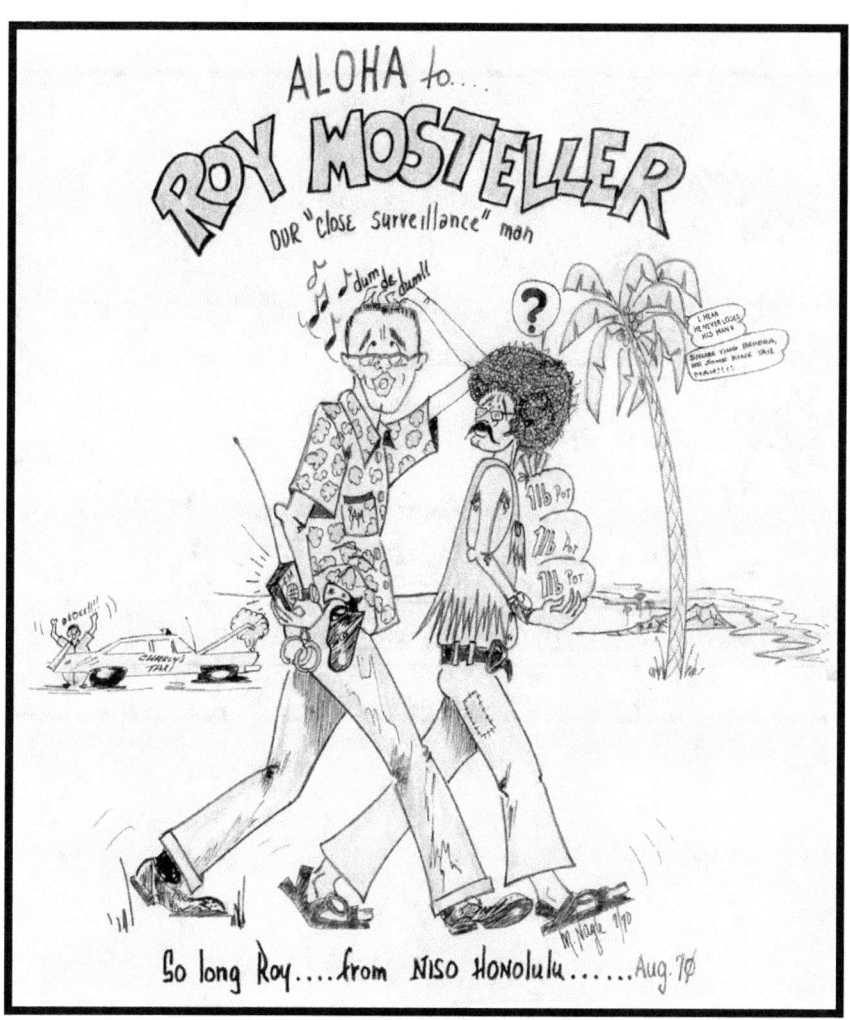

SPECIAL AGENT DON MITCHELL 1972

SPECIAL AGENT FRANK ORRANTIA 1971

CLYDE ROACH, NISPAC 1973

SPECIAL AGENT BOB ROBBINS 1975

SPECIAL AGENT GEORGE SLAUGHTER 1973

SPECIAL AGENT AL TATUM 1973

SPECIAL AGENT TOMMY WILLIAMS 1976

SPECIAL AGENT GARY WITTE 1973

www.ingramcontent.com/pod-product-compliance
Lightning Source LLC
Chambersburg PA
CBHW070626220526
45466CB00001B/109